FINDING SHANNON

THE INSIDE STORY

RICHARD EDWARDS

PRESS·DESK

FINDING SHANNON
THE INSIDE STORY

Published by Press Desk Limited, 2008

www.pressdeskbooks.co.uk

Picture Credits:
Yorkshire Evening Post: Back cover, pages 97–112, 145–147.
John Rivers Photography: 148–159.

ISBN: 978-0-9561268-0-1

Printed in Great Britain

CIP Data
A catalogue for this book is available from the British Library

For the good people of Dewsbury Moor

RICHARD EDWARDS is 33 and has worked as a frontline news reporter in East, North and West Yorkshire for a decade. He has covered huge stories such as the 7/7 bombings, and was one of the first three local journalists to visit Iraq in the weeks following the 2005 elections, but, he says, that none of the events he has covered have been in the same league as the Shannon Matthews' saga. He felt that such a staggering story deserved to be told, in full, by the person who was there from day one and who was privileged enough to be given the trust of the good people of Dewsbury Moor. Richard is a senior reporter at the Yorkshire Evening Post, and his love for Middlesbrough Football Club comes second only to that for his wife and son. He lives in North Yorkshire.

Acknowledgements

Thanks are due to my employers, the Yorkshire Evening Post, all the great people who work there, and to all the members of my huge, weird and wonderful family. Top of that list, of course, are my amazing wife and son, who have had to make do with me vanishing from time to time over the last few months. But a special thank-you and message of respect goes to Dewsbury Moor and all the people who live there. Without their help and hospitality this book would not have been written. What they, and everyone else, should remember, is they did themselves proud when one of their own went missing. Their solidarity stands as an example to others.

CONTENTS

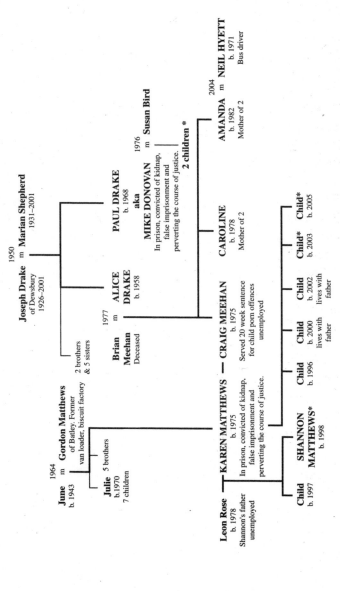

Joseph Drake m **Marian Shepherd**
of Dewsbury   1931–2001
1926–2001

1950

June m **Gordon Matthews**
b. 1943   of Batley. Former
van loader, biscuit factory

1964

2 brothers
& 5 sisters

Julie 5 brothers
b.1970
7 children

Brian
Meehan
Deceased

m

1977

ALICE
DRAKE
b. 1958

PAUL DRAKE
b. 1968
aka
MIKE DONOVAN
In prison, convicted of kidnap,
false imprisonment and
perverting the course of justice.

m **Susan Bird**

1976

2 children *

AMANDA m **NEIL HYETT**
b. 1982   b. 1971
Mother of 2   Bus driver

2004

Leon Rose
b. 1978
Shannon's father
unemployed

KAREN MATTHEWS ─ **CRAIG MEEHAN**
b. 1975   b. 1975
In prison, convicted of kidnap,   Served 20 week sentence
false imprisonment and   for child porn offences
perverting the course of justice.   unemployed

CAROLINE
b. 1978
Mother of 2

Child
b. 1997

SHANNON
MATTHEWS*
b. 1998

Child
b. 1996

Child
b. 2000
lives with
father

Child
b. 2002
lives with
father

Child*
b. 2003

Child*
b. 2005

Children's names have been withheld for legal reasons.

* Away from home, being looked after by others

7

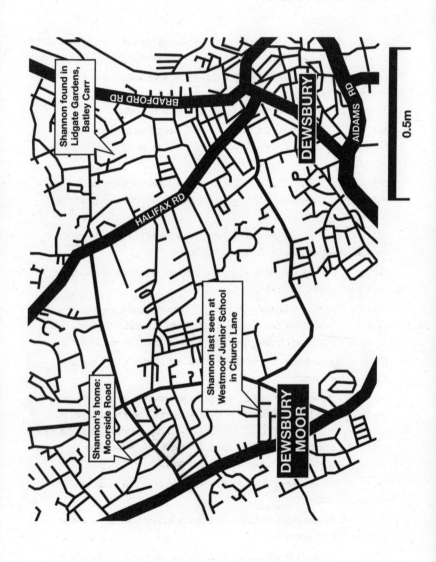

TIMELINE

February 19: Shannon leaves Westmoor Junior School, at 3.10pm. She is later reported missing by her mother, Karen Matthews.

February 20: Police appeal for information on Shannon, saying they are "concerned for her welfare". A search involving 200 officers begins. Shannon's schoolfriends make a video appeal on YouTube.

February 21: More than 250 officers and 60 detectives are on the case. Police report several unconfirmed sightings, and more than 200 houses are searched.

February 22: Police release CCTV footage of Shannon taken the day she was reported missing, as well as pictures of her pink and grey Bratz furry boots.

February 23: Police begin dredging a pond behind Dewsbury hospital. Special constables search Dewsbury Moor.

February 25: Fifty specialist officers search bins on the route between Shannon's school and home.

February 26: A coordinated search of 2,000 houses and open areas is carried out, and 1,500 motorists are interviewed. Around 100 people join Shannon's family and friends in a vigil. Flowers are laid outside her home.

March 1: Karen Matthews makes an emotional Mother's Day appeal for her daughter's return.

March 4: One-tenth of Yorkshire police's operational strength are now deployed in the hunt for Shannon - the biggest such operation since the search for the Yorkshire Ripper. Sniffer dogs trained to find human remains search more than 500 houses. Police build up a DNA profile from Shannon's schoolbooks and other personal items.

March 5: Police release a tape of the 999 emergency call made by Shannon's mother.

March 14: Shannon is found alive in a flat at Batley Carr, about a mile from the family home.

March 17: Michael Donovan, the then 39-year-old uncle of Meehan, is charged with the kidnapping and false imprisonment of Shannon. He is remanded in custody.

April 2: Craig Meehan is arrested and charged with possessing child pornography.

April 6: Karen Matthews is arrested on suspicion of perverting the course of justice.

April 9: Matthews is remanded in custody at Dewsbury Magistrates Court charged with perverting the course of justice and child neglect.

April 11: Meehan is refused bail on charges of possessing child pornography.

September 5: Donovan and Karen Matthews appear in Crown Court together for the first time. Both deny charges of kidnapping and falsely imprisoning Shannon. They also plead not guilty to perverting the course of justice.

September 16: Meehan convicted of 11 offences. He is sentenced to 20 weeks in jail but walks free on time served. Police drive him to a secret address.

November 11: Donovan and Matthews go on trial at Leeds Crown Court.

CHAPTER 1

THE USUAL late morning business was being done in the Yorkshire Evening Post's sprawling second floor newsroom in that iconic, yet shockingly ugly, pile of concrete that sits on the edge of Leeds city centre, glowering at passing motorists while its tower tells them the time and a slightly unreliable air temperature. Phones rang constantly, the buzz of chat, conversation and interviews hanging in the air like pub cigarette smoke in the days before the ban, bursts of laughter seeming to ping around in the building's strange acoustics, popping up in one corner then being flung across the room to another.

Bruce Smith, veteran YEP crime reporter since the days of the Yorkshire Ripper, sat opposite me, his hushed tones barely audible as he chatted conspiratorially to one of his under-the-counter police contacts. The huge pile of old newspapers on his desk, occasionally culled, was so high that morning that I could only just make out his spectacles and the tips of his moustache, moving up and down as he spoke.

The chair to my right was vacant, as Debbie Leigh, a glamorous member of the YEP's younger guard, had run off on a story a few minutes earlier, but to my left, Howard Williamson, one of the last true "gentlemen of the press" with nearly fifty years' service to his name, was rattling away at his keyboard, racing to meet the deadline for that day's paper. In his mid-sixties, but looking at least a decade younger, Howard's secret seemed to be teetotalism, vegetarianism and fasting during the day, allowing only black coffee and fruit juice to pass his lips until the sun went down. Judging by the number of empty plastic coffee cups near his right hand, a small army that was beginning to invade my section of the long, all-in-one desk, it had been an especially busy morning.

My own day had been fairly run-of-the-mill so far, a fire in a derelict building, an appeal for witnesses to a car crash, a you-couldn't-make-it-up tale about British Gas bombarding a man with bills months after he had died, despite his family telling the company of their loss. It was all important, bread-and-butter stuff for a local evening paper, but nothing that would call for the front page to be held.

Journalists on early or late shifts must regularly check with the emergency services for an update on any incidents that might make the news, and just after eleven that morning I began my latest round of calls. The different services vary greatly in how much they tell the media, West Yorkshire Police have a keen and active press and public relations department, regularly releasing stories about the force, while their counterparts in North Yorkshire, to put it mildly, have traditionally taken a lower-key approach - the words 'blood' and 'stone' spring to mind.

To save them from having to deal with bucketloads of calls from journalists, most services communicate with the media through a voicebank, or medialine system, updated by their press officers with recorded messages about incidents. At about 11.20 that morning, I rang West Yorkshire Police's medialine. There was a short and simple new message: a nine-year-old girl, Shannon Matthews, had gone missing from her home in Dewsbury Moor, an estate in a former mill town about ten miles from Leeds. Shannon had not returned home after a school swimming lesson the previous day. There was a description of her and a promise that a photo would be issued as soon as the investigating officers could borrow one from her family.

The way the police described the girl brought home just how small and vulnerable she would have been in that miserable February weather. She stood at just over four feet tall and had her hair in that traditional schoolgirl style, the ponytail. Freckles surrounded her blue eyes. She was dressed in her black school jumper and trousers, a coat with a fur-trimmed hood, and was wearing pink and grey furry "Bratz" boots.

Stories about missing persons nearly always get covered by the regional press, radio and television, which are able to relay the appeal for help in tracing them directly to the community. Like all other incidents passing across a newsdesk, however, each missing person story is judged on how urgent and how newsworthy it is. People don't realise just how often children and young adults go missing from home in this country, often for days or weeks on end. While local newspapers will always report an appeal for help to trace a child, the story always attracts more attention if it is the child's first time away from home. Shannon had never been missing before and, at just nine years old, she was quite a bit younger than many repeat runaways. As West Yorkshire was in the middle of a particularly cold spell at that time, the danger was obvious.

I flagged up the story to my immediate boss, news editor Gillian Haworth, and we ran it in that night's paper. I also put a report onto the YEP's website, and, after I had chased the police for the photo, got ready to head for Dewsbury Moor. Until a couple of weeks earlier, we'd had a reporter, Neil Hudson, permanently based in Dewsbury and the story would have been handed to him, but the post had been scrapped and Neil moved to the features desk in the Leeds office, so, as I had taken the first call, the job fell to me. 'Another Madeleine McCann?' a colleague asked me, as I gathered my things, the mystery surrounding Madeleine's whereabouts still dominating the headlines months after her disappearance. I shrugged, 'Let's hope not.'

The weather was dry, and beautifully bright, but shockingly cold. There had been a deep frost the night before, and as I drove out of Leeds, past the Elland Road football ground towards the Dewsbury Road, I watched as pedestrians walked quickly, woolly-hatted heads hunched into their shoulders, desperate to get out of the biting wind and into the warm.

The grime from the road-salt had formed a film on my windscreen, obstructing my view, but I had to wait a minute or two as I drove to wash it off, the spray-devices stubbornly refusing to work after freezing solid. I shuddered at the thought of spending several hours trudging around in those temperatures. Then I remembered I was off to investigate a story about a little girl who might have been out in it all night. I turned up the heater and drove on.

CHAPTER 2

DEWSBURY'S IMPOSING Victorian town hall and the fine stone houses on the town's outskirts, testify to its former importance as a bustling and prosperous mill town. However, its days as the capital of Yorkshire's Heavy Woollen district - named for the heavy blankets and army uniforms made there by blending new wool with recycled "shoddy" - are now long gone, and the town has struggled to find a clear identity since. Extremist groups have tried to capitalise on divisions between the white and Asian communities but, happily, a concerted effort by the whole community appears to be turning that particular tide.

I had been there several times before on stories, covering for the local reporter when he was on holiday or helping out when extra manpower was needed, and that was surprisingly often - for a small town, Dewsbury certainly generates more than its share of major news. The reason for that is a mystery, and a regular source of debate in the newsroom, but the big stories come out of the town thick and fast,

The Yorkshire Ripper, Peter Sutcliffe, was questioned at Dewsbury Police Station, and formally charged before the Dewsbury magistrates in 1981. Much more recently, in June 2005, a girl of twelve was charged with grievous bodily harm following the alleged attempted hanging of a five year old boy from the Chickenley estate east of the town, and the following month, it turned out that Mohammad Sidique Khan, the ringleader of the UK's first ever suicide bombing unit, the attackers responsible for the 7/7 London bombings in July 2005, had made his home in the Lees Holm district of Dewsbury.

Although I was familiar with the town itself, I'd never been to Dewsbury Moor. As an old-fashioned, and relatively low-waged, reporter, I didn't have the luxury of a sat-nav in my ageing but still reliable Ford, but after checking the A to Z, I saw I should follow the road west past the beautiful landscaped grounds of Crow Nest Park, almost into Heckmondwike.

Having been brought up in the north-east, and covered communities with mainly working class residents on both the YEP and my previous paper, the York Evening Press, I reckoned that I knew my way around council estates fairly well and had got pretty good at guessing how things were on any particular estate after a brief look at the place.

I drove slowly into the Moor, and a quick look told me that this was one of the better-off council estates. Since the Thatcher years and the Right-to-Buy policy, the term "council estate" has become outmoded, but, even in property-price obsessed Britain, there are still people who see their house as a home, rather than an investment, and are happy to live in it in return for paying a reasonable rent, hoping that their local authority will keep its side of the bargain as a responsible landlord, and keep the homes in decent condition.

At first sight, Kirklees Council appeared to have been fair to Dewsbury Moor. There had been recent investment in the estate, many of the homes had been renovated and the surrounding streets converted into Scandinavian style home-zones, giving pedestrians not cars the priority, with bollards and narrow roads that look like pavements to slow motorists down and encourage kids to play outside again.

As happens when you give people something to take pride in, the Moor's residents seemed to be looking after their estate. The place was generally tidy, and most of the homes and gardens looked in good order. Of course some homes had been neglected, and there were scattered signs of poverty like broken toys in a front garden or smashed glass in one of the communal areas, but on the whole, the Moor was in good condition. Some of the estates I've worked on in Leeds would eat it for breakfast and still be hungry afterwards.

Bordered by stone built terraces that date from Victorian times, and with a stunning view of the foothills of the Pennines, on a summer's day Dewsbury Moor might even pass for picturesque, but that Tuesday was far from summery. I found Moorside Road in amongst the winding home-zone streets, and parked the car. As I got out, I was met by the full force of the icy blast blowing straight off the hills down into the valley where Dewsbury Moor lay. As I walked towards Shannon's home, about two-thirds of the way along the street, I could only hope that her trail was not as cold as the wind battering her home on that bleak February day.

CHAPTER 3

SHANNON HAD NOW BEEN MISSING from home for more than twenty hours and by this time, a knot of journalists had gathered and were standing around outside the house, blowing on their hands and stamping their feet to ward off the cold. They were not just those from the local press, but the northern staffers for the nationals, among them former YEP colleague Paul Jeeves, now with The Daily Express, and The Sun's veteran reporter Alistair Taylor. The mood at this point was relatively easy-going, both amongst the news men and women and the locals. There was concern that a girl was missing from home, but the general feeling was that she would be back soon. Who wants to believe the worst?

There was no sign of Shannon's mum, Karen Matthews, or step-dad, Craig Meehan, but Craig's sister, Amanda Hyett, and her husband, Neil, were in the street and happy to talk to the press. Their mood was relaxed in general, probably sharing the view that Shannon would be home in a few hours.

Neil even felt able to crack a crude joke, nodding at Amanda and shouting to the reporters: 'Get your wallets out lads, only a fiver a feel.'

'Shut up Neil,' she said, giving him a playful slap that would have felled a smaller man, while the press pack gave nervous, half-fake laughs, a bit taken aback but not wanting to make our first local contacts feel awkward.

The couple's willingness to talk was both welcome – we all had a job to do – and slightly surprising. Entering a new estate, it can take time and hard work to win the locals over. People everywhere are suspicious of outsiders, and on top of that journalists have to deal with being ranked alongside, if not slightly lower than, politicians and estate agents. In other words, at the rock bottom of the pile. Such an early sign of hospitality and co-operation was rare but if replicated by the rest of Shannon's family, friends and neighbours, would make our work on their doorsteps both easier and more comfortable.

Around the adults and journalists, street life was continuing as normal. Children, some of whom should have been at school, played on their bikes and asked questions of the press. A group of three young mothers walked by with young children in pushchairs, one of them sporting dyed bright red hair and, despite the cold, a top cut low enough to display a huge, gravity-defying cleavage.

'She's paid for them, so she's going to get her money's worth and show them off,' one of her friends laughed, reading the minds of the newcomers.

Amanda told us how her husband had been among a group of Shannon's relatives who had been up until 4am that day searching for her. It must have been an uncomfortable quest, the stress of looking in vain for a missing child made worse by the coldest night of the year so far. With the wind chill factor, the temperature was said to have dropped to minus nine that night. Amanda also described Shannon to us: a quiet girl who loved her family, and enjoyed spending time at home in her bedroom, playing with her beloved Bratz toys.

Significantly, she added that no one had expected Shannon to run away. 'Her brother, is the one for running away. Not Shannon. She's never done it before. No one can work it out.'

In the background, the police operation was getting into full swing. Mounted officers had sealed off Crow Nest Park and parts of the surrounding area, and, as we stood outside the house, word reached us from our newsrooms that Chief Superintendent Barry South, Divisional Police Commander for the Kirklees area which included Dewsbury, was to give a briefing close to Shannon's school, Westmoor Juniors. That school, in Church Lane, was the spot where Shannon had last been seen, nearly twenty-four hours earlier.

By now, the media pack had grown larger and there was a stampede for our cars. The Madeleine McCann story was still very much in the headlines, with no sign of "compassion-fatigue" as yet. Through no choice of her own, Maddie was already a household name. As I drove out of the estate, I wondered if Shannon might be about to join her.

Soon after we reached the school, Commander South and West Yorkshire Police press officer Andy Smith, arrived to greet a group of about twenty-five reporters and photographers. Mr South, a tall man in his 40s with a prominent Roman nose, greeted the pack with the slightly awkward air of an officer who, like many of his colleagues, had spent years treating the press with suspicion, but had been given media training on reaching higher rank. He clearly understood the need for relations with the press, but dealing with us appeared to be far from his favourite task and he was determined to stick grimly to the script rather than reveal anything that might give the story even more human interest.

These days, most uniformed police refuse to speak to the press at the scene of an incident, instead repeating the mantra 'You'll have to call the press office'. Some officers will speak in private, to a trusted reporter, while senior officers, usually detectives, will sometimes speak at the scene. Mainly, though, they have been conditioned to believe that the press will only "twist" what they say. I find that suggestion bizarre. I have certainly never twisted anything; if I did, it would only – understandably – lead to a refusal by that source to ever speak to me again and possibly to legal problems. For me, the "twist" accusation has become just another part of the background noise in an ever more media dominated world. People speak to the press for all sorts of reasons, but more and more of those in the public eye use the media to advance their own personal agenda and, if the public reaction is hostile, they then make the knee-jerk claim that they have been misquoted, or their words "twisted" or "taken out of context".

It's like a game, between press and public, but most ordinary people, either enjoying their moment in the media spotlight, or to be genuinely helpful, will speak. Those that won't are usually persuaded, if the story is good enough, by the tabloid reporter's wallet. That is not an option open to me or my colleagues on the local press. We never pay for stories – some local papers barely pay their staff – so if someone has spoken to me, they have done so for their own reasons, without being tempted into it.

Mr South's terse statement "revealed" that more than 200 police officers were already searching for Shannon, that the local police training school had been temporarily shut so the trainees there could help in the search, and that police were 'extremely concerned' for her safety. And that was about it.

Questions rained in. Had any of Shannon's belongings been found? Were officers speaking to local sex offenders? Was there the possibility that Shannon had been abducted? Did she have a mobile phone with her? Wanting to keep minds focused on this being a missing person's inquiry, and stave off any speculation, Mr South batted most questions back with the line 'Our priority at this moment in time is locating Shannon safe and well'.

Reporters dashed off to file their story, some to phone it through to newspaper copytakers – usually women wearing telephone headsets, highly skilled typists whose fingers whirr across their computer keyboards – other reporters giving the news directly to their viewers or listeners through live television and radio broadcasts. I rang my story through from my car, parked on the slope at the top of Church Lane.

A son to collect from nursery, I headed for home after handing over to late duty reporter, Suzanne McTaggart. Suzanne took up her post outside Shannon's home, waiting for an appearance from either of her parents. She was still there at about 8pm, when Karen Matthews returned from the police station, where she had spent the day being comforted by officers and other family members.

Asked by the press pack to give a quote, to pose for a picture and appeal for her daughter's return, Karen obliged, begging 'Shannon, please come home', through huge, red-ringed eyes and a face that seemed etched with trauma and sleep deprivation. It would have taken a hard-hearted person to see those images and fail to feel for the clearly desperate, distraught woman whose face peered out from them.

CHAPTER 4

DEWSBURY MOOR is an old-fashioned sort of place. It is a place where people know their neighbours on much more than nodding terms; where people look out for each other and help one another. That's not to paint the place in sepia tones or look at it with misplaced nostalgia. Its residents would be the first to admit the Moor has some problems, mainly the sort of stuff linked to bored kids you can find anywhere, estate or suburb, but two factors have stopped things deteriorating as badly as they have in some places, such as the ex-pit villages just a few miles down the road from Dewsbury.

The first is that most of the Moor's residents work – Julie Bushby, chairperson of the Moorside Tenants' and Residents' Association, put the figure at eighty per cent – and the second is that heroin and crack cocaine have not taken hold there, at least not in the way they have elsewhere. That much was obvious even before speaking to the locals about it, as the grey, lifeless and listless look of a place and people gripped by smack was absent from Dewsbury Moor. No doubt there are a few users around, although in my long days there I did not see anyone displaying the telltale signs, and so the life, which heroin greedily sucks away, is still there on the Moor.

Heroin and crack do not just affect people addicted to them, they hit the whole community: families stressed by their loved one's addiction; residents worried their home or car will be targeted by someone looking for easy cash; communal spaces abandoned to dealers and their customers. So far, the Moor has resisted this. The strong community spirit there will keep up the fight against it. That community spirit is embodied in the thriving Moorside Tenants' and Residents' Association. Regular trips and events are organised for the local kids and their families, and the whole estate turns out for the annual August gala.

Chaired by Julie, a bustling, no-nonsense mother of three, who was as fierce in protecting Shannon's family from unwanted intrusions as she would had it been her own child, and she was one of the driving forces as, on day two of the search, the association, known as the TRA, began flexing its muscles. Where the first evening had seen a few family and friends out pounding the streets and fields, doing their best, by the second day the houses surrounding Shannon's home were all displaying posters appealing for information. The influence of the Madeleine McCann campaign was clear. At that time, nearly everywhere in Britain seemed to have a poster asking for help to find the McCann child. You'd struggle to spot one now, the fact she is still missing seemingly erased from our collective memories.

My first story about Shannon had been easy, it wrote itself in a way: she was missing; her family was distraught; they needed our help to find her. Walking onto the estate for a second day, I wondered how I would find the follow-up I needed for the next day's paper. Repeating the appeal for information was no good. Reporters are under pressure to find a "new line," a way of taking the same story forward that, ideally, has not been used by any other media.

The posters were an obvious first option. I asked a passing woman about them, and she muttered a few words then walked on, her coat collar turned up. I didn't blame her. It was dry, yet freezing. Not for the first time, I was relieved that I kept an "emergency" hat and pair of gloves in my bag all year round. If there were decorations in the accessories world, they'd be up for a George Cross for the sterling service they provided in Dewsbury.

I tried a knock on Neil Hyett's door. It whipped straight open, as he was behind it, putting his shoes on. He looked pale and drawn. After searching for Shannon until 4am on Wednesday morning, Neil and close friends, including Pete Brown, a genial Liverpudlian inevitably nicknamed "Scouse", had been in Leeds and Bradford until 10.30pm on the Wednesday night, handing out hundreds of the Shannon leaflets. They had been printed "on the house" by local business owners, while taxi firms gave the free use of cars, coaches and even a double-decker bus to those involved in the search.

A bespectacled coach driver, slightly overweight and sporting a goatee beard, Neil seemed reasonably aware of the workings of the press and had a decent quote to hand. He was also good at remembering reporters' first names. This familiarity led to him being held up to ridicule by some members of the media – and the occasional local cracked a good-natured joke at his expense – but I found him to be friendly, more intelligent than he was given credit for and fairly well informed about what was going on. Neil said he was in a rush to dish out more leaflets, but made time to answer a few questions, giving me the line I needed: 'The police have asked us not to search like we did on the first night, because we could be trampling over forensic evidence. But we have to do something.'

In the background were scenes that the locals were learning to live with – large numbers of police, in fluorescent yellow jackets, looking in bins, in sheds, knocking on doors or holding straining dogs at the end of their tethers. Unless you are a football supporter, or a regular demonstrator, you will not see police in large numbers on a regular basis on Britain's streets, while some people, harking back to days long gone, say you never see a police officer on the street at all, so the sight of scores of uniforms, sometimes walking in formation, through one small area, is both striking and slightly unnerving.

As is the British way, the vast majority of the locals took it on the chin. They believed they were co-operating with these restrictions on their liberty, allowing their privacy to be invaded, for the much greater good. However, after police removed an old mattress from his back garden, Neil was already the subject of a piece in a daily tabloid newspaper that was almost salivating over the fact. Like one or two other people on the estate, it made him the subject of a cruel whispering campaign, falsely suggesting that he might have had something to do with the disappearance.

CHAPTER 5

EVERYONE WANTED SHANNON TO BE FOUND SAFE AND WELL, and that included the media pack gathered at the estate. Despite the low opinion many people have about the press – it mainly seems to be the print media that get the stick – the people working within it are, by and large, decent human beings, who also have families and mortgages or rent payments, just like nearly everyone else. Newspapers sometimes have lapses of accuracy or taste, but less often than popular myth would suggest, and when they do occur, they are often punished in the courts for them.

Of course there are some idiots working in the media, and some ridiculously overblown egos, but that's hardly unique; the same could be said of any industry. Journalists also often resort to some very black humour – a coping mechanism similarly used by members of the emergency services who also come face-to-face with some of the very dark sides of human life – but most understand the situations where the joking must stop and be replaced by respect and professionalism.

People often assume the press want to speak those who are unable to think or make decisions for themselves, or that reporters hound people to make them talk. Although that may sometimes happen, people are often very keen to speak to the papers, for various reasons, and those who are quickest to condemn journalists for trying to get a story are often the first to pick up the paper or flick on the television for the latest update.

As the press pack maintained its vigil on the Dewsbury Moor estate and the unavailing search for Shannon continued, her mother, Karen, and her stepfather Craig Meehan, had yet to speak publicly, still being interviewed in depth at Dewsbury Police Station. A few miles away, their friends and neighbours strained their minds and their muscles to search for Shannon, united in their determination to bring that little girl back home. Amanda Hyett, acting as a spokeswoman for Karen, told reporters she was staying with a friend, had not eaten for days and her eyes were 'red and raw from crying. We are all fixated on getting Shannon home,' Amanda said.

One parent who had been seen in public was Shannon's natural father, Leon Rose, a stockily built father-of-four, who lived several miles away in Kirkburton, near Huddersfield. With a pale, almost grey complexion, and large, dark rings around his eyes, Leon's appearance caused some raised eyebrows, although he looked that way simply because, as he said, he had been spending every available second searching for his missing daughter.

Leon admitted that problems between him and Karen, including rows over money, meant the weekly contact he once had with his daughter ended in summer 2007, but he revealed that, the day after Shannon went missing, Karen had told him the girl had written on her bedroom wall that she wanted to live with her dad.

Leon's thoughts were given added weight after a packed West Yorkshire Police press conference released CCTV stills of Shannon, captured just after she left a swimming class at Dewsbury Baths. Detective Superintendent Andy Brennan, head of the Shannon inquiry, played down the writing on Shannon's wall, saying her bedroom was covered with 'childish scribbles', but, seemingly desperate for hope, Leon said he believed Shannon had decided to come and see him after she left the baths.

As Leon again pleaded for information, Detective Superintendent Brennan was blunt about his own thoughts, saying he was surprised Shannon was still missing. 'I would have expected her to be located by now,' he told the press conference. 'I could not be more concerned.'

Chief Superintendent Barry South also revealed that none of Shannon's belongings, or any of her clothes, had been found by officers searching for her. The search remained huge. Officers on foot and horseback scoured the Dewsbury Moor area, checking any areas that remained untouched and re-checking those that had. A specialist team used ropes and climbing equipment to delve into the murky depths of a storm drain, while relatives, such as Graham Howgate, married to Karen's cousin, Susan, used his dog to carry out touching but seemingly hopeless searches of public areas, such as a corner of Crow Nest Park once known as "lion's den".

'I know it might be a waste of time,' Graham said, 'but I can't just sit there, I need to be out doing something for Shannon.'

Clues, though, remained stubbornly few and far between. As one police source remarked to me, 'We're at the stage where we are shaking tree after tree in the hope that something will fall out. That's all we can do.'

CHAPTER 6

THE LOCALS' ADMIRABLE EFFORT at co-ordinating the search for Shannon was heavily influenced by the global search for Madeleine McCann. The media's coverage of Shannon's story was not. On the face of it, pretty much the only similarity between the two girls was that, at that time, both were missing and had distraught families searching for them.

Apart from that, their worlds were so far apart they could have been from a different planet. Maddie was from a professional, photogenic family, blessed with money, a home in middle-England and the backing of slick media management. Shannon was from a northern, working class estate, was estranged from her father, five of her brothers and sisters had different dads and her press coverage was being handled by determined yet inexperienced friends and family.

At the time Shannon vanished, Maddie had been gone for months, yet the media was still awash with coverage of her story. She was a household name. In those early stages, Shannon was far from that and, while many people would have been aware a child was missing, her plight did not dominate the bulletins in the way the younger girl's did.

That, coupled with the patronising and occasionally vicious tone of the coverage by some of the national media, infuriated me. Nowhere was that more pronounced than in some depictions of the Dewsbury Moor estate on which Shannon lived. It was as if every prejudice against poor, white, working class people, and the estates where they made their homes, was being vented.

There are "sink estates" of course, but far fewer than tabloid headlines would sometimes lead you to believe, and most estates, wherever they might be, are home to hundreds – or thousands – of friendly, genuine people, most of whom have a tale to tell if someone takes the time to listen. Many of them face frightening poverty in their daily lives, but they get on with life, stoically doing their best for their families, working long hours for poor wages, battling to make ends meet, parents going without so their children don't have to, while the pirates of the catalogue and credit market constantly circle, looking to collect the £1.99 a week their clients will often be paying back for the rest of their lives.

Some respond to that poverty by committing crime. Most do not. But when the criminals are caught and rightly punished, that seems to make it open season in some quarters to pillory not only the offenders but all the others in their community as "scum", or that vicious word, "chavs". It's interesting that this does not happen when, say, a businessman in a wealthy suburb is convicted of defrauding huge amounts of money from his place of work.

Those using such labels are generally sneering outsiders who have never met, nor attempted to understand, the people at whom they are throwing such abuse. They might do worse than remember that it was Britain's working classes that built the prosperity of the country, successfully defended it in two world wars, and, by and large, created the wealth that allows a different section of society to live in comfort.

Almost from day one of the Shannon story, much venom was directed towards the people of Dewsbury Moor. One national broadsheet's website described the community as 'home to some of the worst elements of the white underclass'. As I read that, I wondered how many other estates that journalist had visited, how long he'd stayed in Dewsbury, and whether he would have written that line so readily had Dewsbury Moor's population been mainly black or Asian.

As a local reporter closely involved with the case, I was asked to appear on Radio 5 Live's Breakfast programme to be interviewed about the latest developments and, when presenter Sheila Fogerty asked me about the contrast between coverage of Maddie and Shannon's situations, I took the chance to comment about the tone of some of the media coverage. I got no further than the words, 'It's a disgrace…' when I was cut off and the interview terminated, but at least the point had been made.

The story of Shannon's disappearance had not, as some news stories do, started feeding upon itself, changing from day to day, even hour to hour, with editors desperate to be first with the latest developments. Instead, Shannon was mentioned in some places almost as an afterthought, and, as the first full week passed, people were privately starting to say they believed she was dead. This was causing an element of fear to start creeping into the Dewsbury Moor area, every parent's worst fear that someone was on the loose who was an extreme danger to their children. Such predators are, thankfully, extremely rare, but as a society we have allowed ourselves to become more and more paranoid about them; paranoia fuelled by the way the tabloids cover people convicted of offences against children. On the Moor, where one of their children had been missing for nearly a week, locals had good reason to be worried.

Certainly the precedents were not good. Older heads in the YEP office pointed to local examples like Leanne Tiernan and Sarah Harper. Leanne was sixteen when she abducted in Bramley, Leeds, in November 2000. Her body was not found until the following August, in a shallow woodland grave where it had been buried by rapist and killer John Taylor. Choirgirl Sarah was just ten when she went missing in March 1986. Her body was found in the River Trent a month later, where it had been dumped by triple-murderer Robert Black.

Pensioner Thelma Jackson, who lives on the Dewsbury Moor estate, reflected those concerns when I spoke to her. 'It has gone very quiet on the estate, you aren't seeing the kids running around and that's because people are scared, they want to keep them in so they know they are safe.' Thelma also spoke of the pain she was feeling for Karen. 'I don't know how that poor woman is coping,' she said. 'If it was me, I wouldn't be able to think or sleep. My heart goes out to her.'

Karen herself was still yet to speak publicly since the emotional television appeal she made on Shannon's second night away. I was desperate for an interview with her or Craig, or preferably both, but when I finally did come face-to-face with them, even though only a few feet away from them, I was unable to share even a word of conversation.

CHAPTER 7

FINALLY, THERE THEY WERE. Some of the assembled media – me included – were not entirely sure what Craig and Karen looked like, but, when they emerged from number 24 on that freezing, late February day, the relatively small press pack of ten reporters and photographers that was still keeping the vigil outside their home were left with no doubt.

The door suddenly opened and two figures emerged, squinting slightly in the bright sunshine. The wind that day was blowing at almost gale force, taking the already low temperatures down to somewhere close to freezing point, but Karen and Craig kept their jackets open to display the "Have You Seen Shannon Matthews?" T-shirts that were being worn, even though by only a small number of people, across Dewsbury Moor.

They made an unusual looking couple. Craig, a short man, his features hidden behind thick glasses and his trademark baseball cap, his mouth slightly open to display a damp bottom lip and vacant expression that hid his status as the more articulate of the two. Karen was expressionless, her face a pale grey colour, like the cheap soap bars left on the sinks in some public toilets, topped with pale red hair scraped back from her forehead, red rings still visible under her eyes. This trip was the first time they had ventured out in daylight hours for some time, and it was to be a short one, Julie Bushby escorting them to the Residents' Association community house in nearby Moorside Avenue.

Shutters clicked and whirred, but reporters had been told the couple had been asked by the police not to give any interviews, so, biding my time, I decided to introduce myself, gently, letting the couple know I was from the local paper. This can sometimes sway reluctant interviewees, even more so if they are from a core readership area, as Dewsbury Moor is for the YEP. 'Hi Karen,' I said.

'It's Richard Edwards from the Evening Post. We're all thinking of you.'

She didn't reply and that was all I wanted to say at that time, then I quickly backed off. Some of the national photographers ran after them, getting in front and in their faces, but this provoked the expected snarl from Julie. I'd already seen she was a woman not to be messed with, but it wasn't only that which stopped me from following Karen and Craig. I was being patient, playing the long game. Why risk missing the big prize for the sake of shouting a couple of questions only to be told where to go?

Julie had noticed that I, and my photographer colleague, Sarah Washbourn, had backed off. At that point, Julie and I had already had a couple of brief chats, and she, along with residents' group colleague Gemma Alderson, had invited me into the community house for a hot drink on condition I put my notebook away while I was in there. It was a welcome respite from the bitter weather.

As always, Julie was just inside the back door of the community house and any media people who tried to get in, film or interview without permission got a full-on tongue lashing, but fortunately for me, my polite approach, plus the help and coverage the YEP had given to the Search for Shannon campaign up to then, was paying dividends. 'We're having a meeting at one o'clock to talk about what we're going to do,' Julie said. 'Come if you want.' She even smiled as she said it.

I didn't need to be asked twice. 'Definitely, thanks, I'll be here,' I said, pleased but slightly surprised. 'What do you think the chances are of Karen and Craig posing for a picture?'

'I'll ask them,' Julie said. 'But you can't speak to them directly. They've been told not to by the police. If you do try asking them any questions, you'll be out on your ear.'

That sounded fair enough to me. At about twenty-to-one, Sarah and I arrived for the meeting. Julie was not there at that time, and, without her, no one seemed sure what to do, the atmosphere slightly awkward. The community house is a standard semi on the Moor estate, but turned over for use as an office. Its front garden has been paved over, and the front door is kept permanently locked. The back door leads into a small kitchen, where Gemma was usually to be found at the hot water boiler, turning out brew after brew. A door led through into the sparsely decorated front room, used as an office and meeting room. There was a television in the corner, with a rolling news channel on mute. Hundreds of the Shannon leaflets were piled on a table and a small settee near the back wall.

The small room was packed. Craig and Karen were both there, as were Neil and Amanda Hyett, and Craig's cousin, Ryan, among others. As a reporter, it was frustrating being in the same room as Craig and Karen, yet not able to speak to them, at least about Shannon. Craig was generally quiet, but Karen seemed more relaxed than I'd expected, chatting away and sometimes even laughing with the others in there. I thought that slightly strange, but I told myself that different people deal with extreme trauma in different ways. After all, who was I to say how someone should be behaving when their daughter is a suspected abductee, possibly even a murder victim? By this time, the possibility of Shannon being snatched was being discussed, even among those closest to her, with Graham Howgate, the husband of Karen's cousin, among the first to raise it.

The couple knew we were there for a picture, and, with a few minutes to spare before the meeting, I asked them to pose for us outside the house. They agreed, but stayed where they were, Craig silent, Karen chatting. The last thing I wanted to appear was pushy, but if I missed this chance there would be no picture and neither I nor my bosses would have been happy.

I decided to be slightly more direct. 'Come on then you two, let's get this photo over and done with,' I said, trying to reassure them that it was no big deal. Thankfully, they got up, posed outside, and a couple of minutes later the shot was in the bag. Job done.

Just before one o'clock, Julie arrived and the meeting got

underway. Progress had been made with the campaign. A special bank account had been set up for donations. All those involved with the campaign had already put their own money – as well as just about every waking second – into it, and donations were needed to cover expenses. The Moor's locals had been giving generously, but, as they were mainly working people on low wages, the fund total at that point was in the hundreds. It was a telling contrast with the Madeleine campaign fund, which was being measured in the hundreds of thousands.

I felt slightly awkward in the meeting, an intruder even, despite my invitation, but where I knew I could help was with advising the campaigners on how best to keep the story in the spotlight. I explained the press's need for the "new line" on the story every day, and came up with some ideas that they could use to feed the hungry media.

No one in that room was openly talking about Shannon not coming back. They couldn't. For the sake of the campaign, they had to stick solidly to the line that Shannon would be home very soon, whatever their private beliefs.

However, most people are well aware that when a child does come to harm, in the overwhelming majority of cases, the person responsible is someone close to them. In that context, there was a very awkward moment after a particular comment from, Neil Hyett, an honorary uncle for Shannon. 'No one knows where Shannon is,' he said. 'Any of us could have her. I could have her for all we know.'

He was only saying out loud what everyone must have been thinking: that the answer to the terrible mystery could be right under the noses of those trying desperately to solve it. Until then, no one had dared to say it and some sharp looks were directed at him. It was at an extremely sensitive time, and Neil, utterly wrongly, had already been on the rough end of some questionable reporting about the mattress story from a national newspaper, but whether my journalistic antennae were over-sensitive at that time or not, I was sure I detected a split-second of hesitation among those there, and his comments certainly seemed to hang in the air for a second or two.

The meeting went on, and I was encouraged by the fact that everyone was not only tolerating my presence, but seemed to welcome my ideas. As the meeting was wrapping up, Neil, even praised the job the YEP had done. 'We can't thank the media enough so far,' he said. 'And especially the Evening Post. I say we should make Richard our first point of contact on this, the YEP have been brilliant so far.'

It's rare to get praise like that even in a situation that is much less intense than the one we found ourselves in, so, understandably, I left happy, feeling like major progress had been made from a reporter's point of view. Unfortunately, there was nothing doing with the story I really wanted to write, the story that said Shannon had been found, safe, and was coming home. Detective Superintendent Brennan was by now admitting an abduction was a line of inquiry, and officers had resorted to setting up roadblocks and stopping cars in the hope someone had seen something, anything. While both the police and the locals were doing all they could, the chances of Shannon being found alive were starting to look as bleak as the weather.

CHAPTER 8

AS THE NUMBER of days Shannon had been missing passed into double figures, the police began to say what many people had already been thinking – that there was a chance she was dead. While stressing that the West Yorkshire force was still officially carrying out a missing person's inquiry, and hope had not been given up that Shannon would be found alive, Detective Superintendent Brennan told a press conference that the search had taken on a different tone and now had the style of a murder probe.

As well as experts in search techniques from the National Search Centre, who had been on board from the early days, specialist body search dogs were also drafted in from Greater Manchester Police. The dogs were similar to those deployed in the grim search for human remains at the former children's home in Jersey at the centre of abuse allegations.

Back on the Moor, residents had seen what appeared to be the first signs of "community justice" against those suspected – on the back of little or no evidence – of being involved in Shannon's disappearance. Locals and reporters were astounded to hear that a 43-year-old man from Dewsbury Moor had been found "crucified" outside his home, his hands nailed to a home-made cross. Rumours instantly started to fly around: 'Shannon was in his flat'; 'He knows where she is'; 'He's a well known local paedophile'.

Shocking and bizarre though the incident seemed at first glance, it turned out not to be nowhere near as serious as it first appeared. The man's injuries were relatively minor, no evidence was ever produced that he was any sort of sex offender, and police said there was no link between the incident and the search for Shannon. No one was ever arrested in connection with the "crucifixion," and the man was quietly moved off the estate amid rumours – some coming from within West Yorkshire Police - that he had somehow managed to inflict the injuries himself, an attention-seeker looking to force himself under the microscope that was focused on Dewsbury Moor. The man himself was never traced by the press, and it seems the full truth about the story may never be known.

Although some papers were starting to use that well-worn phrase 'feelings are running high', the reality on the Moor was that the people there were generally calm, united in their determination to get one of their own back. Regular candlelit vigils were being held, with large crowds gathering on Tuesdays outside the community house to show solidarity for Shannon. More meetings were held to discuss the next move for the campaign, though ideas were starting to run slightly short.

Just about everywhere that could be leafleted had been, nearly every Dewsbury business and thousands of homes were displaying the Search for Shannon posters, and local sports clubs, such as Leeds United, Bradford City, Huddersfield Town, Dewsbury Rams, Batley Bulldogs, Bradford Bulls and Leeds Rhinos had donated memorabilia to raise money for the fund and had made appeals for information before the game.

The "Find Shannon" campaigners needed some inspiration and the timely arrival of an annual event provided it. Mother's Day was the perfect opportunity to call for help to bring home a missing child, provided Karen could be persuaded to talk. Although she was officially still not speaking publicly, West Yorkshire Police worked with Karen to prepare a statement.

Broadcast on Mothering Sunday itself, and widely published the following day, Karen told the world's media: 'Mother's Day is a day every mum wants her children around them. I don't want cards or presents, I just want my darling daughter home safely. I know Shannon would normally have made me a Mother's Day card at school and we would have spent the day together. I have a special bond with Shannon and I feel sure that she is alive and will come home to her mum. If you or anyone knows where Shannon is, please think about my family this Mother's Day and bring my beautiful princess home where she belongs with her mum, dad, brothers and little sister.'

After watching Karen's broadcast, Julie Bushby told me: 'Somehow, she seems to be bearing up well. But I know that she has a private moment every day where she goes off for a cry, and that helps her cope. I don't know how she is doing it. I don't think I could.'

That Mother's Day press statement proved to be a tipping point for Karen. Until then, she had uttered few words on the record or in public, and that statement, on a day which must have seen mothers around the world united in sympathy for her, must have taken some nerve to prepare and then release. But as the days wore on after Mother's Day, she definitely became more confident before the cameras and the notebooks, and less than 24 hours after Mothering Sunday, she felt brave enough to place herself onto the global media stage.

CHAPTER 9

SPEAKING DIRECTLY TO KAREN or Craig, but preferably Karen, was the story, or "scoop," to use a classic, old media term, that pretty much every journalist in the country was now chasing. A serious missing child case, as Shannon's had been for some time, would nearly always see an appeal from one, or usually both parents, pretty early on. That we had not yet heard from Karen was unusual and West Yorkshire Police's press office, particularly their Kirklees area press officer Andy Smith, was being deluged with calls about Shannon, many of them asking when Karen would be speaking.

As I had found, Karen and Craig had been asked by the police to keep quiet in the early stages of the search, but, as the two-week anniversary of Shannon's disappearance approached, the way was cleared for her mum to go public.

By this stage of the story, the big media guns had embraced it and Moorside Road had taken on an entirely different look. Broadcasting vans, with mobile television transmitters, were parked up and down the street, with the odd radio car, fitted with a smaller mast, dotted amongst them. Sky News had gone as far as setting up a table outside Shannon's home, used for their presenter's bits and pieces, which gave them a feeling of permanence in the street. Like the Americans on military operations, Sky were the best kitted out of all the broadcast media, down to the padded boiler-suits their off-camera staff used to keep out the cold. They looked odd, but style counts for nothing when you're trying to cope with hours of standing around on freezing, windswept streets. Shivering, despite my several layers, I looked on enviously. In the same field of vision I could see one TV team doing a live broadcast, another discussing the latest developments, a third gulping down much-needed hot drinks and a fourth touching up the presenter's make-up.

While the broadcast media camped on the side of the

pedestrianised street closest to Shannon's house, the print media were a few feet away, on the other side of the path. Photographers and reporters tended to group together, and it was heartening to see there were few, if any, airs or graces shown from the national press towards their local counterparts. They knew that the local knowledge and contacts of a colleague from the Dewsbury Reporter was the likeliest source of the juicy bit of new information everyone was looking for.

With a press pack that size, rumours were seized upon hungrily and spread like warm margarine, so when word got around that Karen was to give a press conference, the reaction was a sight to see. Like an alarm call among a family of meercats, the news galvanised everyone into action, their first instinct to grab their mobiles and try to ring the West Yorkshire Police press office. Of course, the line was jammed, as hundreds of press people tried to find out what was going on.

Unusually for the West Yorkshire force, it was a piece of poorly handled public relations. It turned out that rather than enter the bearpit of a full press conference, Karen would instead give a "pooled" interview to the Press Association, a news agency which sells its stories to whichever paper wants them, not printing any publications itself, and to one nominated camera crew. In that way, she would effectively be speaking to the world. Whoever wanted that interview would be able to print or broadcast it.

Whether this was Karen's decision, or taken on police advice, was no more clear than the reasons for the breakdown in communication between the force and the media which led to a crazy stampede from Dewsbury Moor to the town centre police station, with all the reporters psyching themselves up for the closest they were likely to get to a one-on-one interview with Karen.

My own reaction was one of dismay at first, thinking my softly-softly, build-it-gently approach to winning Craig and Karen's trust had been wasted, wondering if I had taken too long and lost the story as a result. I was also concerned about missing the press conference.

Despite the police medialine not carrying a message about it, as the man on the spot, it was my job to know what was going on, and, rightly, my bosses would not have been happy had a conference gone ahead without me in it. Relief swept over me as I was halfway between the Moor and the town centre, when I got the message that the session was being pooled. The relief was double, first, I hadn't missed the big story, and secondly, whatever came from the conference would dominate the next day's paper, giving me some breathing space to find my tale for the day after. Several reporters must have got a similar message as they hared off towards town, as mine was not the only car doing a U-turn halfway down the Heckmondwike Road then getting back to the Moorside as quickly as possible.

I watched the interview at home that night. Karen told the Press Association's reporter, Dave Higgins, that she cried herself to sleep every night, and that she could not bear to go into her daughter's bedroom. Throughout the interview Karen blinked back tears, the odd one escaping and trickling down her tired-looking, pale face, and she clutched Shannon's favourite teddy-bear, treating it like a security blanket, as she recalled how her daughter's last words to her had been, 'see you at teatime Mum, love you.'

When I spoke to Dave Higgins the next day, he said Karen was so upset after he asked what her daughter's last words had been, that he was ticked off by Michelle Flint, the police press officer handling the interview.

Inevitably, the main attention was focused on Karen, but Leon Rose, Shannon's natural father, had also made another statement. Leon, said he had kept up his daily searches for his daughter. Other than that, he was struggling for words, and when asked what he though had happened to Shannon, summed up in a few short sentences the bafflement everyone was feeling: 'I have no idea. All I know is that she went to go home from school and didn't go home. That's basically all I know.'

The interview with Karen made headlines on every news bulletin and every newspaper. Reading the stories that came from it, and watching the television footage, I thought Karen came across well. She had also said she believed someone was holding Shannon, and that she could no longer trust the people closest to her. I interpreted that as a line the police had fed her in an attempt to flush out the real story. It was another sign they believed the answers still lay within Dewsbury Moor, a belief they emphasised by keeping their search teams concentrated on a relatively small area surrounding Shannon's home, doggedly continuing to turn over stone after stone, and shake tree after tree, looking for the break that would lead them to Shannon.

CHAPTER 10

BY NOW, I was well into a Shannon story routine. Everything else I had been working on was well and truly on the backburner, Dewsbury Moor being the only show in town. I'd get to the office for about 7.45am to check my emails and landline voicemail, to see if there were any hints or tip offs that would help take the story on.

After my daily bowl of porridge from the staff canteen, I'd check my kit. Reporters, unlike photographers, can usually travel pretty light. A notebook and a pen is all you need, maybe a tape recorder, but they're not for me, as I tend to find they make the person you're talking to clam up.

This job, though, needed a bit more kit. Firstly, I was making sure I had at least four pens with me (I usually carry two) because the cold was stopping them working, but most of my extra equipment was clothing. On the coldest day yet, I was wearing a vest, shirt, two jumpers, thick parka jacket, scarf, hat, gloves and two pairs of socks. Fussy about not "feeling the benefit" of the extra warmth if I wore this in the car on the way to the job, it was all packed the night before, then, as I arrived on the Moor, I'd get into the back and put all the extras on in a flail of skinny arms and legs. If any coppers had been going past, they'd probably have had a look through the steamed-up windows, thinking they'd caught a couple with a taste for al fresco fun.

After the kit checks, I was off on the route I now knew so well, swinging past Billy Bremner's statue outside Elland Road, the air so cold you could imagine him steaming around the pitch in his heyday, breath flaring from his nostrils. Onto the ring road, past the Environment Agency offices where I'd covered meetings that were crucial for local news but a million miles from this in terms of excitement, and then onto the Batley road with the newsagents where I'd often stop for a freshly cooked samosa to keep the winter chill at bay. I drove down the big hill towards Dewsbury, where I could put the car in neutral and coast to the traffic lights, passing the innocent-looking woman who was at the same spot, every day, having a hugely animated conversation into her mobile phone. One day, I thought, I'm going to stop and politely ask her who she speaks to at the same time, in the same place, every day. I crawled past the station, stuck in a small jam at the lights, and itching to be back on the Moor to get on with the story. Then I turned onto the Heckmondwike road, with beautiful Crow Nest Park on the right, serving as a headquarters for the police mounted section during the inquiry. Past Church Lane, where Shannon's school stands, I took a sharp right turn and drove into the estate, through the home-zone streets and into my usual parking spot on Moorside Avenue, outside the community house, a minute's walk from Shannon's.

I chose to park there for a couple of reasons. One was access. The news crews all seemed fixated on parking in Moorside Road, as close to the Matthews house as possible, but that meant a nightmare manoeuvring in and out, and there were times, at the end of a long, busy, freezing day, I just wanted to be away. Secondly, there was a respect thing. Our presence was hard for the locals, and, though they dealt with it admirably, taking all their parking spaces was hardly going to endear us to them. I also thought it was inappropriate for some of the better-off journalists to be parking flash motors on what was a pretty poor street. That didn't apply to me, a local man on a local paper wage, I drove a battered, second-hand Ford, but some of the freelance photographers, in particular, were obviously doing rather better and were turning up in Jags and BMWs.

That particular morning, March 4, Andy Manning, the YEP's picture editor, had come up with an idea. He knew I was building up trust with Craig and Karen, and suggested I ask if we could take some pictures inside Shannon's bedroom, a guaranteed front page story that would give strong publicity to the search for her.

I weighed up my chances. I had been in the same room as

Shannon's mum and step-dad a few times now, and we had exchanged a few words, although I had been very careful not to ask anything too direct about the search. I wasn't entirely sure they trusted me enough to let me into their home, but, knowing she had done those recent interviews, I knew I had a chance. There's always a chance. Being a reporter is all about asking the awkward, cheeky or unexpected questions, and you genuinely never know how people will react. Even after more than a decade in the job, I'm still amazed what people will tell me.

On the estate, I was told that Karen and Craig were already in the community house. Our photographer, Sarah, was waiting for me and we walked over to the house together. Julie and Gemma greeted us, Gemma pouring us a brew, for which I put a few coins on the collection plate. More and more people were gathering in the house each day, all wanting to do their bit, but also all wanting a drink – and drinks need to be paid for. I was glad to see plenty of coins on the plate.

Craig and Karen were in the midst of it all, dressed in their Shannon T-shirts, Craig quiet, busying himself with search plans for that day, Karen noisier, flitting between the living room, kitchen and outside, to smoke cigarettes, chatting to the others in the room. The way she was behaving didn't strike me as quite natural for a mother whose child had been missing for two weeks. Unlike her appearances in front of the cameras, there was no obvious strain on her face that day, and she was smiling and laughing as she shared a smoke in the garden, not appearing too concerned with the next move in the community's efforts to find her daughter. In fact, at that point, she was taking no interest whatsoever, while Craig, on the other hand, stood looking confused, holding on tightly to a bunch of Shannon leaflets. Once more I reminded myself that different people react to stress in different ways, and I had no idea what was going on in Karen's mind, even though outwardly she might look relaxed and cheerful.

I started a stilted conversation with Craig and Karen, Craig the easier of the two to chat with, as Karen sometimes seemed to struggle with her words. This was explained to me later when I found out her reading skills are pretty poor. The ever-popular male subject of football worked with Craig, a Manchester United supporter, but for Karen, then in everyone's mind a woman in turmoil, small talk didn't seem appropriate. Instead, I tried to talk about how she was coping, asked what it was like doing the interview with PA, whether there had been any news from the police. I spoke about the way we had handled the coverage in the YEP, a story every day, before taking a deep breath and asking Karen the $64,000 question: 'How would you feel about us doing some pictures in Shannon's bedroom? It'll definitely get on the front page and really help publicise the search,' I said, more in hope than expectation.

Quickly, and after barely thinking about it, Karen turned to Craig and said: 'We could do, if it'll keep the profile going.'

'Yeah, I think so,' Craig said. 'There's the new bedding we've got ready for when she comes home.'

I could barely believe my luck. For a reporter, this was the equivalent of a footballer scoring the winning goal in a vital cup-tie. Although writing the story, and seeing it on the front page with your byline underneath, is a great feeling, for me it doesn't compare to the moment you know the big story you've been chasing is in the bag. A buzz like that is the reason journalism is such a great job, and it's just as good every time you feel it.

CHAPTER 11

DESPITE BUZZING INWARDLY, outwardly I had to stay calm and respectful, reminding myself I was dealing with a traumatised couple. I had been invited into somebody's home, and so, of course, I would behave with courtesy, but this home was also one which was torn apart by worry, so I would be treading extra-carefully, thinking about every single word so as to avoid any risk of upset.

As with that first picture nearly a week ago, Craig and Karen needed a bit of gentle nudging before they were ready to leave the community house. This was a crucial point – our deadlines meant we had to get cracking, but a word or two in the wrong place here could have meant them changing their minds. Slowly, we moved out of the back door, along the side of the community house and up the short, windy and quite steep path connecting Moorside Avenue and Moorside Road. The path snakes past several gardens, with low fences offering no privacy. In one, a woman in a vest top was hanging out her washing despite the bitter cold, then we passed a run-down play area before reaching the penguin-shaped bollards close to Julie's house. As we turned left, the other members of the press pack caught sight of us, no doubt wondering what was going on, but for some reason, none asked any questions as we walked past them up to number 24.

The front of the house was unremarkable. Like all in Dewsbury Moor, it had a small front garden, the grass slightly overgrown, the white, UPVC front door having gone a shade of grimy grey over time. The door had been left unlocked, and next minute we were inside.

I glanced around, trying to get a mental snapshot of the house they shared. Immediately through the front door were the stairs, pairs of shoes on nearly every step, to the left was a door marked by dirty fingermarks close to the handle. It led to the living room, occupied by

Craig's cousin and one-time best friend, Ryan Meehan. He seemed a genuinely friendly, easy-going lad, his demeanour in contrast to his height, burly build and the large scar that dominated his prominent forehead. As we chatted, he told me that he spent hours on end at Craig and Karen's, baby-sitting the children when they were out, surfing the internet and playing X-box games with Craig. He was usually to be found on Craig's computer, tucked away in the corner of the room. It was a recent replacement for Craig's original, which had been taken away by the police to see if Shannon had left any clues in emails as to where she might be.

Another computer, Karen's, was to the right-hand-side of the living room door. On the wall next to it, were pinned messages of support, sent into the home from strangers. Several of them were from media organisations or individual journalists, offering words of sympathy, all signing off with offers to listen to the couple's story. An old trick, and one I'd used myself in the past.

There were two settees in the room, one near Craig's computer, the other at right-angles to it, facing the deluxe-size television which can be found in most estate homes. Underneath it were a DVD player and the X-box. Dominating the chimney breast was a huge portrait photograph of Shannon, her younger brother and little sister, Craig's child with Karen. When I paused to look at it, Karen told me that it had been taken on Shannon's ninth birthday and was one of only three or four pictures of her eldest daughter that she possessed.

Through from the living room was a sparse, gloomy kitchen, where their dog, Scania, was skulking around, wearing a classic hangdog expression. Bizarrely, Craig told me that their pet had been named after an advertising slogan for Netto supermarket: "Scandinavian for value". The kitchen smelt of dampness and cigarette smoke, and there was a chill in the air. When I mentioned to Karen that the dog looked sad, she said: 'She's been like that since Shannon went missing. Her and Shannon get on really well, she knows something is wrong.'

I asked Karen if she was ready to take us to see Shannon's room but, saying she couldn't cope with going in there, she sent Craig up with us instead. Blinking behind his thick glasses, Craig, as ever, seemed unfazed, and led Sarah and I up the stairs, the carpet covering them a thin, worn brown. He stank of body odour, something I'd noticed on our previous meetings too, and made me wonder why those closest to him didn't say anything about it. The stench was so strong that there was no way that Karen at least could have missed it, yet he always seemed to smell that way.

Four doors opened off the landing at the top of the stairs, all painted white but grey with age and smeared with grubby marks. The bathroom door was partly open, the next two firmly shut, and the fourth wide open, as if waiting for someone to return. This was Shannon's room. If anyone was in any doubt, the names of Shannon and her little sister and the warning "Keep Out", had been scrawled on the chipped, plywood door in the schoolgirl's childish hand.

I asked Craig how his little girl was coping. The answer was painful to hear. 'She doesn't understand as much but she is starting to realise Shannon isn't here. Every morning, we hear her calling out for her sister.'

The room itself was a mini palace of pink and fluffiness, sprinkled with dolls and soft toys, Shannon's Dalmatian print dressing gown was hanging off her top bunk, ready for her to put back on. The garment was so tiny it was a stark reminder of just how young, small and vulnerable this missing child really was. Shannon's beloved Bratz toys had been stored on the top of the wardrobe, for safe keeping, but Craig said that her little sister had claimed Shannon's favourite teddy, curling up with it every night for comfort.

I took the opportunity to ask Craig for his mobile number so that we could keep in touch as things developed. As we chatted, I noticed Karen had quietly come to join us. I found that surprising, given what she had said, just a few minutes ago, about not being able to cope with going into Shannon's room, but from the point of view of the interview, I was glad. As we talked, Sarah took her pictures, showing great skill by managing to keep the sometimes intrusive art of photography quiet and discreet, even somehow seeming to mute the click of the shutter.

When I asked Craig how he was dealing with the situation, he instantly welled up with tears, the first time I had seen real emotion from either of the two of them. He told me that his dad had died just four months earlier, his auntie a couple of months later. 'I don't think I have got my head around losing my dad yet, so we are all trying to keep each other going,' he said, the tears getting closer to spilling out.

Karen then told me Craig was the strong one of the couple – 'He's been a rock for me' – before, quite harshly I thought, telling Craig to keep himself together. 'Don't you dare cry now,' she told him.

While the ways of the new man, the man who is allowed to show his emotions, have yet to fully make their way into heartland Yorkshire estates, I remember thinking that a cry was probably just what Craig could have done with at the time. Karen then seemed to remember what she had said earlier. 'Anyway, I can't be in here,' she said and then disappeared downstairs.

Finished in the bedroom, and not wanting to upset Craig further, we followed Karen down to the living room, where an update of the Shannon story was on the news. Everyone gathered round, the volume turned up high. It was a strange experience, the lines between the story and the newsgatherer feeling blurred at that point.

Before leaving, I asked Karen how she was coping. 'Wherever I am, the stress is always there,' she said. 'I toss and turn at night, I can't sleep properly. We think she is out there somewhere and that she is going to come home. It's that thought that keeps us going.'

CHAPTER 12

THE SEARCH FOR SHANNON had now become West Yorkshire Police's biggest operation since the search for the Yorkshire Ripper, an inquiry that began in the mid 1970s and was not concluded until Peter Sutcliffe was jailed in the early 1980s. YEP crime reporter Bruce Smith loves to be reminded that on the night I was being born, in October 1975, he was out on the streets of Leeds, covering the aftermath of the first Ripper killing.

The comparison between the two inquiries was made in an unguarded moment by a senior detective talking to a YEP reporter. The policeman was referring to the amount of manpower being used, rather than any direct similarities between the circumstances, but, understandably, the comments were seized upon by every newspaper covering the story and all the broadcast media.

Sutcliffe is in competition with Moors Murderer Ian Brady for the title of Britain's biggest bogeyman, with Ian Huntley, currently held in Wakefield Prison, in the running to take over when one or both of them finally breathe their last. So any story involving the Ripper, no matter how ridiculous, is gold-dust for the press – a car crash story for readers and viewers who pretend they don't want to look, but, in reality, they can't help themselves and are morbidly fascinated by what they see.

Those Ripper comments forced the police to put out a public statement, with press officer Tony Tierney relaying words from high up the chain of command asking reporters to back off from comparisons with Sutcliffe, making the valid point that Shannon's was still a missing person inquiry. However, in terms of manpower if nothing else, the comparison was probably accurate. Armed with Shannon's DNA and fingerprints, obtained from her family and her schoolbooks, ten per cent of West Yorkshire Police's entire operational strength was now out looking for her. That huge number of officers, more than 250 uniformed officers and 85 detectives, had already searched 500 homes in the Dewsbury Moor area and planned to visit 2,500 more.

There had also been another slight shift in the police's position. Detective Superintendent Brennan was by now saying that while officers still hoped to find Shannon alive, they had no choice but also to explore the theory that she had come to harm. It was hardly necessary for off-the-record sources within the force to confirm that the search had become a murder inquiry in all but name.

The community still stuck to its line that Shannon would be coming home. It had to, although there were moments, when, understandably, thoughts of the worst did slip out. Mark Aldridge, dad of Shannon's best friend, Megan, visibly shook when he spoke about seeing CCTV pictures of the missing girl, with his daughter alongside her. Like many others at that time, he believed Shannon had been abducted. 'It could have been Megan,' he said. 'But I'm trying not to think about that. We are concentrating on Shannon coming home.'

Mark, a softly spoken man, clearly devoted to his daughter, had a gentle manner contrasting sharply with his career as a professional fighter, competing in the "ultimate fighting" championship. At his Dewsbury home, the other side of the Heckmondwike road from Dewsbury Moor, with a large pen containing his beloved Staffordshire Bull Terriers in his back garden, he spoke about the effect Shannon's disappearance was having on Megan. His daughter had struggled with building friendships, Mark said, but he had been relieved to see her make two friends, one of them Shannon, but then 'One of them went to Australia and now Shannon vanishes. It is unbelievable. Since it happened Megan has been having trouble sleeping and she is finding it hard at school.'

When Megan came in, I asked her if she had any message for her friend. 'Please come home, Shannon,' she said. 'We have all been really upset since you went away.'

A few hours after Craig and Karen had opened up their daughter's bedroom to the YEP, Dewsbury Moor residents held their latest candlelit vigil. It was the biggest yet, with more than 100 people turning out to support Karen and Craig, as well as each other. People cried openly as Karen knelt down to light the first candle for her daughter. When all the 160 flames had been lit, they spelled out Shannon's name, while Megan released balloons carrying heartbreaking messages calling for the missing girl to return home and asking for information about where she was. Prayers were led by the local clergy and the crowd sang a tear-jerking version of *He's Got the Whole World in His Hands* ... with the words adapted to include references to Shannon and her family.

As dawn broke on another freezing day, a team of officers, aided by a JCB, were deep in the mammoth task of searching through scrubland opposite Crow Nest Park. Anyone who sees glossy television programmes about the police, and believes their job to be glamorous, should have seen this. Wearing dark boiler suits and baseball caps, their police badges giving them an almost paramilitary appearance, the group of ten officers, equipped with spades and garden forks, stood in a line as the JCB lifted, then dropped, a huge pile of dead branches, tangled ivy, brittle-dry undergrowth and filthy, fly-tipped rubbish at their feet.

They then picked through it with their tools and gloved hands, finding nothing, before waiting for the next load to drop. The exercise summed up the search at that point – no one expected to find anything, but the job had to be done to either keep that faint hope alive or to confirm the worst, to relieve those affected of the agony of not knowing.

With no obvious story for the following day, I was relying on my trump card, Craig's mobile number. I'd tried it a couple of times that day, but the phone was switched off. Third time lucky though, Craig answered. Could I come round to talk about a story for the next day?

'Yeah, that should be fine,' Craig said.

CHAPTER 13

THE FACT I'D BEEN INVITED BACK to 24 Moorside Road showed that I'd done my job the day before, without annoying anyone and with luck I would now be trusted to do the same again. Parking in my usual spot, I walked quickly up the path, leaving me slightly out of breath, though perhaps a bit of the breathlessness was excitement, knowing I'd put myself a step ahead of the competition and potentially made stories easier to come by. My confident – or even cocky – bubble was deflated when I knocked on number 24 and there was no answer. I knocked a second time, still nothing. Then, thankfully, Karen's voice, sounding slightly distant, said 'Come in.'

Yet when I opened the front door and walked in, there appeared to be nobody about. 'Hello?' I called, in that strange, questioning tone you use when in someone's home with no-one there to greet you, the uneasiness of being on unfamiliar turf and the feeling you are intruding close to the front of your mind.

Still there was nothing for almost a full minute and I stood, irresolute, in the hall undecided whether I should walk through to the kitchen or just stay where I was until Karen or Craig appeared. Suddenly there was a shout of 'Boo!' from behind me, and I felt fingers tickling my sides. The shout and the unexpected touch made me jump out of my skin. Astonishingly, it was Karen. She had hidden in wait behind the living room door, watched me looking around, bemused and confused, then leapt out to surprise me.

In normal circumstances, I would have laughed it off, and come back with a jokey response, but these were not normal circumstances. Was this really a woman enduring the living nightmare of one of her children being missing?

I managed to force a laugh, which must have sounded horribly fake, and spluttered, 'You got me there, Karen.' Pathetic, I know, but try thinking of something witty to say in a situation as bizarre as that.

Karen seemed to find it funny, anyway, as she was laughing her head off.

What on earth was going on? I had no idea, and just stored it away in my memory, one more baffling occurrence awaiting an explanation, though I told myself that at least it confirmed she was relaxed around me. While I was still floundering after Karen's behind-the-door game, Craig appeared, having just popped out to "the chippy". The house turned out to be pretty crowded because Shannon's younger sister was playing in a corner and there was a Channel 4 film crew camped in the kitchen, making a documentary about the search for Shannon.

I plonked myself down on the settee in the living room, feeling that standing around awkwardly might have made for a strange atmosphere. There was no immediate need to talk, so I sat there watching the television flicker away, the volume on mute, mulling over the strange moments when I had walked into the house. I had brought copies of that day's YEP, carrying the story about Shannon's bedroom, with me to Moorside Road. Handing them over, I kept my fingers crossed that they would go down well. Craig, busying himself with the fish and chips, said he would read it later, but Karen started to look immediately, though the way she flicked through, not lingering on it for more than a couple of seconds, added to my belief that her reading skills were not of the best. Craig then handed his partner a huge portion of fish, chips and curry sauce, and she got stuck into it straight away, pushing the newspaper away. I was slightly taken aback by her healthy appetite, but again reminded myself that stress affects people in all sorts of different ways.

As she wolfed down her fish and chips, Craig told me that more messages of support had been sent to the family, including a very touching one from Madeleine McCann's parents, Kate and Gerry, showing their sympathy and understanding for Shannon's family and friends. it was a godsend for the Shannon campaign, because those few lines sent by the McCanns would generate the publicity that was needed badly by then, to keep the search in the national headlines. Strangely, another message had been sent from a prisoner at Her Majesty's Prison Armley, in Leeds. It was pinned to the wall, though Craig said that neither he nor Karen knew the man.

The Channel 4 crew were now filming us and the room fell silent, apart from the sound of munching. Hunger set my stomach rumbling at the scent of a fish dinner. I wasn't sure where or when to start the interview; I was there for a reason but was seemingly the only person wanting to get on with it, though the delay was encouraging in one way, showing that they trusted me enough to be in no rush to chuck me out of the house. As I sat watching them eat, I remembered that Craig's job was working behind a fish counter and, any port in a storm, I asked him what sort of fish he would recommend.

'Cod or haddock only,' he said. 'Don't touch anything else, the rest of it is all disgusting.' He then went back to his meal. Fair enough, I thought, and kept quiet until they had finished and were busy licking their fingers. Then, to get the interview started, I asked Craig and Karen what they thought about the comparisons that were being made in many parts of the media between the Matthews/Meehan and McCann families.

'They're nothing like us, they're snobs,' Karen said, uncharitably, although that was possibly her inarticulate way of trying to stress that, socially at least, the two families lived in separate universes. Having more power over his words, Craig was more measured: 'The message said they were thinking of us, they are going through exactly the same thing, so they know how we are feeling. We shouldn't be compared to them because they are celebrities in other peoples' eyes, and they have all the money. It is a bit ridiculous.'

That conversation came back to me when McCann family spokesman Clarence Mitchell revealed that people, claiming to be from the Matthews' family, had contacted the McCann family to ask for donations from Maddie's fund, which had now topped £1million. The contacts were made through email and by phone calls, and even led to a discussion among McCann trustees as to whether or not to make a goodwill donation to Shannon's family. However it was decided, Mr Mitchell said, that because of the 'haphazard' nature of the requests, they should be turned down. Had there been a more sophisticated request for money, it might have been granted. It has never been made clear who made these requests, but the person behind one of them, a phone call, claimed to be in the same room as Karen at the time.

During my interview with her that day, Karen raised the subject of donations to Shannon's fund herself, saying that any remaining money when her daughter was found 'will go back into the community. It will be spent on the kids because there is nothing for them to do,' she said.

We also spoke about ideas for the following day's story, a suggestion of taking a picture with Karen and Shannon's favourite teddy bear was knocked back, but a later idea, for a shot with the little girl and Scania the dog, got the thumbs up. Meanwhile, Chris Kiddy, a reporter for Calendar, ITV's local news programme in Yorkshire, had begun to do a live update outside the house. When it flashed up on the screen in the living room at number 24, it prompted a cheer from Craig, Karen and Ryan, for once distracted from the computer screen.

It was a "Truman Show"-like moment and Ryan decided to test just how live it was by waving at the camera. After a second's delay, the wave appeared on screen. More cheers and some laughter. As I prepared to leave, another update on the story began, this time on Sky News. There was a call for quiet as the item reported the release of Karen's 999 call to police the night Shannon had vanished. Of everyone there, Karen appeared to be watching the most intently, sitting right in front of the screen, leaning forward, her eyes filled with tears. Karen's image popped up as her stunted sounding voice was played out, beginning 'Hiya, I want to report my daughter missing, please.'

As this happened, the little girl, sitting on her mother's knee, pointed at the screen, and said 'Mummy'. The tears started to stream down Karen's face, briskly, and without a sound, she brushed them away.

When I watched the Channel 4 footage of me with Craig and Karen, I saw that, while I was speaking to Craig, Karen pulled a face to the camera and complained about me being in the house, even though I'd been invited in. Was this Karen thinking she had to behave one way for one part of the media and another for another? It was another strange sidelight on a strange day.

CHAPTER 14

IT WAS THE ST PATRICK'S DAY WEEKEND, a big occasion in Leeds because of the city's huge and historic Irish population. I was on weekend shift, which meant I was the duty reporter from 10am on Saturday morning until 7am on Monday morning. I was given a list of other jobs to do, but obviously Shannon was the priority, my job to find a story for Monday's paper and to be ready to react should anything happen.

The search had now hit a lull. The media – myself included – were still swarming all over Dewsbury Moor, but in reality things were quiet. I was glad of the brief distraction of the weekend shift, although I did make a trip out to the Moor on the Saturday, where I chatted to Craig. He and Ryan were in, watching television. I joined them for a while, little chat being exchanged, the cousins not seeming to have much to say, but also seemingly happy for me to stay, though my own powers of conversation were not at their best that day. Craig told me he was hoping to persuade Dewsbury boxer Gary Sykes to wear a Shannon T-shirt during an upcoming appearance on Sky television. It was a good idea, but one I heard nothing more about.

I left none the wiser, hoping my trip to see Leon, Shannon's natural father, would be more productive. The town where he lives is surrounded by rolling countryside and fields full of livestock, an easy-on-the-eye contrast to the Dewsbury Moor streets I now knew so well.

I knocked on the door of his house and he emerged from the back a few seconds later, a roll-up cigarette between his lips. He looked ill. Ashen faced, with days of stubble on his chin and huge black rings around his eyes, his appearance spoke of someone who had not slept properly for days. We shook hands and chatted briefly, but while Leon was friendly he would not say a word about Shannon. I got the impression that he had been signed up by another media outlet, a deal which would earn him some money but which would be void if he spoke to anyone else.

During that same weekend, police sources told David Bruce, the YEP's chief crime reporter, that the search teams had recovered several items of interest, including pieces of children's clothing. Detective Superintendent Brennan said that none of the items recovered were Shannon's belongings, but they were being examined to see if there was any link between them and the girl's disappearance. Karen, Craig, Shannon's friends and her schoolteachers were all asked to inspect the items before the police were able to say with certainty they did not belong to her. Karen also spoke to reporters to say she was terrified that police would arrive at her home with Shannon's clothing, and that she did not dare to go searching for her daughter for fear of what she might find.

At a time when there was a growing sense of despair over Shannon, I enjoyed covering and writing about a purely positive story, during my weekend duty. Sunday was the day of Leeds' big St Patrick's Day parade, and while the temperature stayed cold, the sun was shining and thousands of people turned out to join in the craic, from second and third generation Leeds Irishmen to those who just liked the taste of Guinness. I took time to watch the parade, following it through the city centre to look for an unusual angle for the next day's paper. I found one: on one of the floats were about a dozen black people, all recent immigrants to the UK from the Caribbean island of Montserrat. Dressed in several shades of green, they made for a striking sight, so I ran to catch up. It turned out that in the 1600s some Irish settlers had travelled to Montserrat, and these revellers were their direct descendants. St Patrick's Day is a big deal there, apparently, and the surname Irish is as common there as Smith is here.

One of the weekend reporter's duties is to check all the national papers for anything that might be of relevance to your own patch, and of course the Sundays were full of Shannon stuff, the majority recycled from the articles I'd been working on all week. However, one of the Sunday tabloids had what was claimed to be an exclusive interview with Leon, explaining his reluctance to talk to me. Leon said he believed his daughter was being held captive, but still had hope that she would be found unharmed. 'If anyone's holding her, I'd like them to examine their conscience. She's a good lass, she hasn't done anything wrong. I'm sure she wants to go home. Friends and family are missing her, it will do us all the world of good. This nightmare needs to end. I beg anyone who may be holding Shannon – please, please let her go free. She is a good girl. Be kind to her and let her return to her family where she belongs.'

Leon also said he was continuing to search for Shannon, spending hour after hour sifting through a tangled, litter-strewn woodland in the hope he would find some trace of her. He vowed to keep going until his daughter was back home, and said he spent restless nights, constantly waking, wondering where his flesh and blood was. 'I can't bear the thought that we don't know where she is. Every morning I wake up hoping: "Could this be the day we find her?". But the pain goes on. I feel so empty when I go to bed knowing she is still out there and we haven't found her.'

In a separate report, two young lads claimed to have seen Shannon at 3.20pm on the day she went missing, ten minutes after the final confirmed sighting. They reckoned to have seen her sitting on a wall in School Lane, not far from Moorside Road, and said she was crying her eyes out. Police said they were aware of the report, and that the two boys had been interviewed about it.

When their claims were put to Karen, she said: 'It breaks my heart to think she was so upset and we didn't know why. Why did no one comfort her and bring her home?'

CHAPTER 15

THE TRAIL FOR SHANNON SEEMED TO HAVE GONE AS COLD as the average temperature during a day on Dewsbury Moor. The cold was relentless, worsened by the icy winds that blew straight into the estate's streets. Moors can be beautiful, but also bleak, and there were long periods up there that would have tested the endurance of an Arctic explorer. Some of the press pack shivered, others, mainly the photographers, more used to working outside for long spells, seemed hardened to the cold.

Wearing my layers of kit, I kept myself busy to keep warm, never standing around for too long and thinking of story ideas to follow up to keep the body and the mind moving. Others did stay parked outside the house without seeming to go anywhere else, like a young reporter from The Daily Mail, who would turn up infrequently, always just in a suit, never an overcoat but seeming unbothered by the cold, while an equally young counterpart from ITN, similarly lightly clad, was slowly turning blue.

Rumours and gossip were horse-traded all day, the arrival of fresh information causing a ripple of reaction that spread up and along the pack, which was now taking up a 200 foot stretch of Moorside Road. What warmed things up were the locals, showing a continuing tolerance and a welcome that went well beyond the call of duty. By now, most of the press who weren't already acquainted had come to know each other, and were also on first-name terms with many of those in the street. Tea, coffee, cigarettes and chat were on offer from the owners of quite a few homes, Julie Bushby's in particular, kindnesses that won't be forgotten by those who received them. Another kindness was the residents allowing us to use their toilets. The drinks were vital to keep warm but would rush straight through you in those temperatures.

The vast majority of locals were friendly, though not all were glad to have us there. One, not from the Moor, stole a reporter's car, another, who lived in Moorside Road, regularly swore and threatened violence at any press person who lingered too long near his garden fence. A youth threatened to smash the camera when I was recording a television piece in which I was sticking up for Dewsbury Moor in the face of some of the inaccurate and stereotypical knocking pieces that had popped up. Another fell between the two stools, mouthing off to photographers than happily posing for pictures, proudly displaying the electronic tag fitted around his ankle.

Rightly, the locals listened to and shared their own gossip and rumour – this, after all, was about their own community – some of it accurate, some of it as wild as the pieces in the Sunday tabloids. Speculative stories had started to appear in the papers linking Craig with Shannon's disappearance. yet no local ever made such a claim to me, and Craig was backed by Leon, who said: 'I'm horrified anyone would suggest that. They got on really well. I was not around for some years and he has been a real dad to her.'

However, the rumours persisted, with Craig being accused of violently controlling both Karen and the children. Although, again, no local ever spoke of that to me, one woman said Craig had once hit her during an argument, and Karen, for a couple of days during the search, had a black eye. Accusations and implications were made elsewhere, with Karen's mother, June, speaking of a 'sinister presence' in her daughter's house, while her brother, Martin, accused Craig of hitting his niece. In turn, Karen stood up for her partner, saying the claims were 'rubbish' and that Shannon loved her step-dad, while Craig himself denied he had ever hit Shannon or the children, and claimed that June had always wanted to make trouble for her daughter's partners.

Meanwhile, in the background, the police doggedly searched on, the officers sometimes looking weary, rarely even acknowledging the media village backdrop, just doing their job. Detective Superintendent Brennan said his men and women were now putting in fourteen-hour shifts and teams of two or three officers with a dog were all over the estate, checking people's homes, while the locals took the invasion of privacy as a necessity, and were just as dogged themselves, never giving up hope, still arranging events. The latest was a sponsored walk, organised to raise funds for the Search for Shannon campaign, held on the day she had been missing for three weeks.

The Sun had now put up a reward of £50,000 for information, while Leon, speaking of the 'unimaginable agony' he was going through, again urged: 'We want everyone in Britain looking for our little princess.' In an inspired move, designed to banish thoughts of the worst from people's minds, the residents' association got local children to make and sign a huge card for Shannon. Julie said Shannon would be given it when she returned home, holding the line solidly and, without actually saying as much, daring anyone to wobble. 'The way we have to look at it now is if and when Shannon does turn up, we want to be able to show her all the effort that has gone in here to try and find her. Wherever she is, she might not know this has been going on and we want her to know she hasn't been forgotten by anybody here.'

The walk went ahead in freezing, driving rain, Karen, Craig and Leon walking close together, Karen saying: 'Hopefully she will be back next week where she belongs.'

CHAPTER 16

ON THURSDAY 13 MARCH, Karen popped up on Radio 4's Today programme. After the earlier days, when her daughter's plight appeared to have been sidelined by much of the media, Karen, an unmarried mother-of-seven from a northern council estate, was now being interviewed not just on Radio 4, but on its flagship programme. That was how big her story had now become.

After the interview was broadcast, some people said they felt Karen had been harshly treated, and that Sarah Montague, her interrogator, came across as entirely unsympathetic, aggressive even, while Karen did her best to answer questions from a person used to grilling cabinet ministers before she has even had her cornflakes.

In the interview Karen repeated the belief she had expressed to me on the day I first went inside her home, that someone she knew had abducted Shannon. Karen stressed that she had 'no idea' who might be behind the abduction, and said that all her family and friends had been checked, she was then asked why someone close to her would want to kidnap her child. 'Just to hurt me really,' she said.

Once more, I found myself thinking that it was a strange, puzzling thing to have said, unless the words had been put into her mouth by the police, hoping that if a family member was holding Shannon, the pressure would become too much, forcing them to cave in and confess.

That evening, Karen and the rest of the estate got a break from the media notebooks, microphones and cameras. The Residents' Association had organised a disco to raise funds for the Shannon appeal, and reporters were politely but firmly asked to stay away. 'We are grateful for the publicity,' Julie said, 'it is really important, but this is a chance to give people a bit of a break.'

Those wishes were respected and the cameras and reporters stayed away and what happened that night went on in private, the only camera there that of the Residents' Association, used to make a video diary. However claims were then made that, after the disco, Craig had tried to take his own life with an overdose. He was not to be seen next day, but talk of the suicide bid was soon forgotten among the monumental events of Friday 14 March 2008.

CHAPTER 17

EXHAUSTED FROM THE ENDLESS HOURS I'd been spending chasing the story on Dewsbury Moor, I had already convinced myself that nothing significant would happen that day, and was settling down by the open fire roaring in the hearth. I had a fresh cup of tea in my hand and the television was tuned to Channel 4's racing coverage. March 14 was also Cheltenham Gold Cup day; I had followed Denman since his debut race and had now backed him to beat Kauto Star and win the Gold Cup. I couldn't wait to see their showdown. Some hope.

'That's great news,' I spluttered, the adrenaline instantly starting to pump around my veins and the racing forgotten. 'Is she OK? And is it absolutely definite she's been found?' There was no way I wanted to ring people only to have to call back and shatter their hopes later.

'As far as we know she's fine,' YEP news editor Gillian Haworth said. 'And yes, it's definitely Shannon.'

We rang off and, my head spinning, I called Julie Bushby. She normally does her best to keep her emotions in check, but on that unforgettable Friday she couldn't help but show some. She already knew why I was ringing and, before I could get more than a couple of words out, she barked 'Is it true?' down the phone at me, and then repeated it before I could answer.

Trusting my boss – and the impeccable sources of David Bruce – I confirmed it, and at once heard Julie's throaty voice relaying the news to the people with her, followed by loud cheers and screams of relief and elation. I shared that elation. Everybody in the country – and beyond – was glad to hear that Shannon was safe. Having spent so many hours on Dewsbury Moor and with the people who live there, I had built strong relationships, even friendships, with some.

Day off or not, Gold Cup or not, I had to get to Dewsbury Moor to cover, and take part in, the celebrations. As I drove the route I had followed so many times before, I thought about what it would mean to that tight-knit community to get one of their own back. I also thought about how rare it is for a missing-child story to have a happy ending. Yet, the closer I got to the Moor, the more incredible it all seemed. Gillian had told me that Shannon had been just a short distance away from home, in a flat in Lidgate Gardens, Batley Carr, for all that time. Not only that, but she had been found in the home of a man called Michael Donovan, but born Paul Drake, who was far from being a complete stranger. In fact, he was Craig's uncle, the younger brother of his mother, Alice.

All this spun around in my head and I kept wondering how Shannon came to be there and how she could have been so close to home without anyone noticing. Dewsbury and Batley are neighbouring towns, almost twin towns, how had this man managed to keep a nationally-famous missing child in his flat for so long without anyone seeing anything?

Those answers would come later, but for now, it was time for Dewsbury Moor to celebrate an unlikely victory, to drink in the glory of being right all along, that Shannon was alive and would be rescued from whoever was holding her. I pulled into my usual Moorside Avenue parking spot, feeling utterly different from all the other times I had arrived. Before, I had turned up with a job to do, a desire to help the people who were keeping the faith while also reporting the news, good or bad, as I am paid to do. At times, I needed to draw on a grim determination, pushing thoughts of the worst to the back of my mind.

This time, I arrived to a completely unknown feeling. I had spent so much time on the estate, invested so much in the story that, even though I had never even met her, it felt like I knew Shannon. Having been so close to it all I felt entitled to join in with the celebrations, the happiness, I suppose, mixed with a bit of pride that we at the YEP had done our bit to help trace her.

The day Shannon was found was also the first mild, sunny day on the Moor so far in 2008. In a community where people are naturally inclined to spend time out and about, this called for a full-on, al fresco party, and by 2.30pm things were already warming up nicely, three women popping corks and laughing wildly outside the community house.

I walked up the path to Moorside Road, thinking it would be one of the last times I would do so. Seconds later, I was right among the scenes of celebration. Dozens of children, more than had been seen for weeks, ran and cycled in and out of the legs of parents, friends, aunties, uncles, as well as the small army of journalists, shouting, laughing and smiling as they did so. Reporters were interviewing Moor residents, taking down quotes which comfortably wrote themselves. Shannon had been found, it was the only story in town, the only emotion one of sheer joy, perhaps tinged with a little disbelief for some.

Scouse Pete was standing outside his home, a broad grin on his face as he gulped down a can of Carlsberg, and before I could even say a word in greeting he had me in a bear hug, shouting at the top of his voice: 'This man has been brilliant. We can't thank him enough.'

Good for the ego that one, and really nice to be appreciated, but I knew I could not allow myself to get carried away, a combination of professionalism and British reserve seeing to that. 'Thanks Pete. Just doing my job though, glad I could help,' I mumbled. I headed for Craig and Karen's front door, knocked and walked straight in. I had another ego boost as those in the house greeted me with cheers, but then it was back to work, time to find out what people knew, when they had heard. Like all that had come before, it was a strange tale. Natalie Brown, Scouse Pete's wife, had received a text message saying word was going round Dewsbury's Asda store that Shannon had been found.

How the news reached Asda was unknown, but it is likely someone living in Lidgate Gardens, near Donovan's home, worked there and was preparing for a shift when the rescue drama unfolded.

'After the text,' Natalie said, 'I got a phone call, telling me people were talking on MSN about how she had been found. Karen and

Craig hadn't heard anything. It's the best feeling ever – and a big sigh of relief.'

Pete joined in. 'Natalie got a phone call first from her sister, then we got a call from a mate saying they were 99 per cent certain it was right. I told Karen, she hadn't heard a thing. I said to her, "Don't quote me on this but we have had a phone call saying she is safe". As soon as I told her she broke down in shock. It was the same for Craig, he just started shaking. I'm still shaking myself, I'm full of adrenaline, I can't believe it.'

Gemma freed from her tea urn at the Residents' Association, said she had got a text with the news from someone at Dewsbury College. 'We had to keep asking if it was true, we didn't know for definite until you rang. The corks have been popping since then,' she said.

Gradually, the full story started to filter through. As a somewhat distant member of Shannon's family, Donovan had been due a visit from the police anyway, but given the huge and tangled web of relations attached to the Meehan and Matthews families, a step-dad's estranged uncle was not top of the priority list and it had taken quite a while for police to knock on Donovan's door. Getting no answer, officers spoke to a woman living in the flat below, who told them she had heard a child's footsteps in the address above, but, at least as far as she knew, the man living there did so alone. When she also told the police that the man above did not go anywhere without his beloved car, which was still parked outside, big alarm bells began to ring in the policemen's minds.

They called for back-up, and help arrived in the form of a search team who smashed the door off its hinges. Officers burst in and found Shannon in a secret compartment built into a divan bed, with Donovan cowering in the other one. She appeared to be unharmed. As the officers carried Shannon out, neighbours gathered round, asking 'Is it Shannon?'

There were loud cheers when they got the answer they had been hoping, dreaming, and, in some cases, praying for. Donovan, led away in handcuffs, appealed to his neighbours: 'Don't hate me. I'm a poorly man.'

His plea cut no ice with locals horrified to learn the missing girl had been under their noses all the time. They unleashed a volley of abuse at Donovan, who, one witness said, was refusing to walk to the police car, instead curling his legs under him as he cried and whined like a tired toddler.

The twenty-four day search was over. Shannon was safe, her step-dad's uncle in custody, arrested on suspicion of abduction and false imprisonment. After all the effort, and all the huge resources that had been deployed, it was a routine call that had found Shannon, and those – mainly Karen – who had said the culprit was someone close to the family were proved right.

It was an occasion which called for a drink, and Scouse Pete wasn't the only person enjoying one. The whole Moor seemed to be getting stuck in, and rightly so. Cans of lager are common accessories on the estates anyway, but this wasn't the usual daily drinking, this was a working class community, drinking with something to celebrate, and those parties are always ones you want an invite to. People clutched anything they could get their hands on, from low-level lagers all the way up to super-strength brews. Some, including a few women, favoured cans of bitter, others swigged straight from the neck of wine bottles, while still more went for the spirits and mixer in a litre-bottle trick.

After phoning my story through to the YEP, I was ready for a drink myself, and spotted my chance to get a round in for the locals, to say thank-you for their help and hospitality. The corner shop was doing a roaring trade, a queue of smiling Moor residents waiting to buy their celebratory booze. I left with two clinking bags and headed back to the community house, where people had started to gather.

I was confronted by a spectacular scene. The children, what seemed like hundreds of them, had got hold of the boxes of Search for Shannon leaflets and posters and were tearing them into ticker-tape, hurling it up into the air with shrieks of joy. There was so much of the stuff it really looked like there had been a snowstorm, a strange contrast on what was actually a warm day after the bone-chilling three weeks that had gone before. Looking on, drinks in hand, or getting in amongst the snowstorm, were the Moor's locals, and well-wishers such as the community policeman, local councillors and clergy.

I ducked away from the celebrations briefly, wanting to ask Alice Meehan, who I'd got to know quite well, about her brother, Donovan. She told me what little she knew. 'I didn't have much to do with him. I last spoke to him around the time my husband died last November; he helped me through it after he died and did a lot for me. He was good then, I can't believe Shannon was in his flat. We weren't a right close family, he got on with his life, I got on with mine.'

Alice also said she felt that Craig should have taken legal action against Karen's mother, June, over some of the critical newspaper stories. I asked Alice why her brother had changed his name from Paul Drake.

She shrugged. 'He did it just before dad died but none of us knew why.'

Reports later emerged that claimed the name change was done in tribute to the singer Jason Donovan, who Michael was said to have become obsessed with at one point in his life, although no family members were able to confirm that. Later, a more likely theory emerged, which said that Alice's brother was obsessed with the 1980s science-fiction series V, which included a character called Mike Donovan.

Alice couldn't let me have a picture of Donovan, and we said our goodbyes soon afterwards. Her closing words to me were, 'I just want to see Shannon and my son, and I want to know why he (Donovan) has done it.'

Dusk was falling and music was drifting over from the community house, a short distance up the road. The party would go on until 6am the following day, and would involve some serious drinking and dancing, and one of the locals doing a streak along Moorside Avenue, but it was time for me to leave; my wife and son were waiting at home.

I drove off, window down, to waves and cheers from the party, a warm feeling inside. Then it struck me – one last thing. I spotted Steve Riding, a long-serving YEP photographer, and stopped the car to ask him: 'Do you know what won the Cheltenham Gold Cup?'

'Denman,' he said. 'And I backed bloody Kauto Star.'

In the grand scheme of things, it didn't matter a bit. But back then, it felt like the icing on the cake.

CHAPTER 18

I WAS BACK ON THE MOOR by eight the next morning, ready in case there was any sign of Craig or Karen, or, ideally, Shannon herself. Karen and Craig had missed the big party, having spent the Friday night in a hotel, but the place had a genuine morning-after feel about it. A handful of television and radio reporters were filing for the early bulletins, one or two kids circled on mountain bikes, otherwise the place was quiet, curtains drawn. At the community house, nearly all the cans and bottles had been tidied up, packed into bin bags, an impressive job by whoever had managed to do that at the end of the party. Likewise, much of the ticker-tape had been swept up, some of it reduced to a pile of ash from which a thin and acrid plume of smoke snaked up into the fresh morning air.

Vicky and Ian Saunders, who lived a few doors down from number 24, had put up a banner declaring 'Shannon is Found,' instead of the banners appealing for help to trace her that had joyously been torn down. Slowly, people started to appear, Julie Bushby somehow managing to do a live radio interview after just two hours' sleep. 'I was the last one to bed,' she said. 'No stamina, these young ones.'

Later in the morning, Scouse Pete came onto the street, grinning as he sipped from a hair-of-the-dog lager, to be joined a couple of minutes later by Neil Hyett, who was also smiling, pulling a Lambert & Butler from a fresh packet and lighting it up, inhaling deeply. 'I had a good night's sleep for the first time in ages last night,' Pete said. 'I think a lot of people did.'

We chatted about the way the estate had coped with the intrusion, how the searchers had kept their morale up, thinking of ways to keep themselves busy from day to day. Neil was honest enough to admit to feeling frustrated at times. 'Sometimes I just had to go off and walk around the estate for a bit, it felt like we were banging our heads against a brick wall, not getting anywhere. But we always kept our hope, we had to. We had to for each other and for Shannon.'

Peter praised the work done by Julie, Gemma and their residents' association colleagues throughout what must have seemed like a never ending 24 days. 'It was going on a long time but they never gave up, never lost hope, and this is the reward. The way this estate came together during this was brilliant, and I hope it can be kept together now. A lot of stuff was said and written about us, but all the time this was about a nine-year-old girl. Nothing else mattered.'

That nine-year-old girl, though, was nowhere to be seen. Karen had been allowed only fleeting contact with her daughter since she was found, and that had been through a glass screen. No official comment was made on the closed visit, but at the time it was interpreted as a way of stopping any forensic evidence from being contaminated.

It looked like Shannon would be away for some time, but no one doubted that she would eventually be reunited with her mother. Police told the YEP that interviews with Shannon would take weeks, as trained officers, backed by a child psychologist, gently asked the girl about her ordeal. All the answers were being filmed, to save Shannon having to give evidence at any trial, and the interviews were held in a special police suite, designed to look like a classroom. She had even been given a kitten to play with.

People on the Moor weren't questioning the police's need to speak to Shannon. But they had started to question why it had taken the force so long to find her, given that she was such a short distance away, being held by a family member. And they weren't alone in their views. People from outside the Moor were echoing those questions, including the Tory MEP for Yorkshire and Humberside, Edward McMillan-Scott. 'In more than three out of four cases like this,' he said, 'a family member is involved. Police should have conducted a thorough search that would have included the suspect.'

The MEP's intervention chimed with the frustration some locals were feeling, but to imply that the police operation had not been thorough did not sit well with the fact that ten per cent of West Yorkshire Police's capacity had been deployed, that officers were working through a long and tangled list of Matthews and Meehan relatives, and a non-blood related, estranged uncle was only about halfway down it. Nonetheless, allegations were flying, fast and furious, with some people in the Batley Carr area, claiming they had reported Donovan days before police visited his flat. Neighbour Melvin Glew, said he contacted the Missing Persons helpline about his concerns. In turn, a spokesperson for the charity said it had contacted police on March 3, asking them to check an address in Lidgate Gardens. Mr Glew also claimed to have received a recorded message when he rang the police number on the Search for Shannon posters. He said his suspicions were roused when he saw a man calling at the flat, but receiving no answer, after arriving in a car with 'Find Shannon' posters in the windows. That man's identity was not revealed, but unless it was by chance, his visit suggested that someone other than Donovan could have known Shannon was in there.

At times struggling for an original story during the search, I and the rest of the press now had more stories than we could deal with. The police criticisms were interesting, but the top priority was now to get to the family. As the reporter closest to them, I briefly found myself in the strange position of being approached by national journalists, asking if I would be able to arrange an interview. 'We will pay,' one reporter said, his raised eyebrow, serious expression and emphasis on the final word indicating that if the interview went ahead, it wouldn't be pennies going into Karen's bank account or back pocket.

I never got the chance to discover if she'd be interested. Firstly, when I called Craig's mobile phone, it was switched off, and then, unexpectedly, the couple returned home on Saturday evening. The press pack went mad, howling for pictures and firing off questions, but, refusing to be overshadowed, friends and neighbours gathered outside number 24, cheering wildly as Craig and Karen got out of the car, and clapping them all the way to their doorstep.

The interviews would wait, but the pictures were spectacular. First, Karen gave a relaxed-looking smile for the camera, her eyes appearing to shine, the result making her look years younger, almost innocent, then she and Craig shared a kiss.

Karen's relaxed appearance showed that a weight had been lifted off her mind. That was her and Craig's moment, but within twenty-four hours the rumour mill was up and running again, and this time it went into overdrive.

CHAPTER 19

ON MONDAY, MARCH 17, MICK DONOVAN was still in custody and still being questioned, with officers taking all the time at their disposal to try to establish just how Shannon came to be at his flat. Police sources had told the YEP's chief crime reporter, Dave Bruce, that Donovan would be charged that day, but when I clocked on for work at noon I was told that the police had applied for their third and final extension on the custody time available to them. That 36-hour extension, granted by a magistrate, would allow the force to hold their suspect until the very early hours of Wednesday. After that, unless charged, he could walk from the station a free man. The pressure was building, and the tension could be felt even a few miles away from Dewsbury Police Station outside number 24. A huge press pack was still in place, the air crackling with the excitement and anticipation generated by a huge, ever-changing story.

I had started at midday because I was on late duty that week. Late shifts normally run from 2.30pm onwards, but I'd been asked to come in those couple of hours early, and was more than happy to do so, not wanting to miss anything. As it turned out, I had already missed something, but it was only the amusing sight of a big gang of journalists, all desperate to keep on top of every development, turning nothing into something.

Craig and Karen had spent Sunday holed up in number 24, hardly venturing out at all, but the two of them then appeared early on Monday, and were whisked off in what looked like an unmarked police car. My colleague Debbie Leigh, on Moor duty until I arrived, said the reaction was like a bomb going off, with frantic phone calls being made as it went around that the pair had been arrested. Police contacts and the staff in West Yorkshire Police's Kirklees Division press office, manned by a beleaguered Andy Smith, must have been both bewildered and exasperated as their phone lines became temporarily jammed.

Whoever started that particular Mexican wave must have been slightly embarrassed when the couple came home an hour or so later, clutching bags of groceries and a crate of lager. They had been nowhere more sinister than on a supermarket shopping trip. Their bags included some gifts for Shannon, including a Bratz doll, the brand of toy the whole nation knew she loved from the repeated descriptions of the grey and pink Bratz boots she was wearing on the day she disappeared.

I needed to speak to one, or preferably both, of them, but my link inside number 24 had now been cut off. Craig's mobile no longer seemed to be working and a community support officer was now guarding the way into number 24. No reporters, no matter how well trusted, were allowed inside.

In the end, I turned the coverage back on itself, guessing Karen would want to say something about the rumours, which were now circulating, that she herself had been involved in Shannon's disappearance. Friends and family were still being allowed into the house, so I wrote a note suggesting she stand up for herself, speaking out to deny the allegations, and suggested some of the things she might want to say. I gave the note to one of her friends who kindly agreed to take it in for me .

Ten minutes later, the note was back in my hand. Nothing had been added to it, but the friend told me: 'She says that's absolutely fine.' The story was being prepared in much the same way as the police press release of the previous day, but this time it was to be a YEP exclusive.

Towards the end of the afternoon, Craig ventured out to the local shop, just a couple of minutes from the house, but so intense was the media interest at that point, a police family liaison officer had to come out first, to clear the way for a mundane journey that Craig must have made a thousand times before.

While uniformed police officers and community support officers rarely, if ever, give any help or information to the press, liaison officers are generally more relaxed. Dealing with the media is part of their job, and they understand that journalists have their own job to do. Respect and courtesy is nearly always shown both ways.

'Craig's going to be coming out to go the shop in a couple of minutes,' the officer said. No more was needed. By telling us this, he was asking that the press people give Craig a bit of space. He wasn't saying don't take pictures, just take them from a decent distance and don't get right into his face. A similar thing had happened a couple of hours earlier, when Karen made a short trip out with the liaison officers. Knowing the photographers were desperate for a shot, Karen and the police made a slow, staged walk past the cameras, giving each one plenty of time to get their image rather than have to dash around, shoving each other – and possibly those not involved – as they did so.

Craig murmured 'No comment', to the reporters' questions, then walked off around the corner. Surprisingly, no one bothered to follow. Karen had not acknowledged me when she walked past, but I knew I stood more chance with Craig, so, when I thought everyone else was distracted, I slipped off around the corner after him. I met him as he was on his way back from the shop, his hands in the pockets of a blue-and-white ski jacket, his baseball cap, as ever, pulled down over his eyes. Always a slight looking figure, without Karen at his side, he looked childlike and vulnerable, an appearance that contrasted with the level of intelligence I knew he possessed. We shook hands, but Craig clearly didn't want to stop. He did, however, answer a couple of questions, telling me he was stressed but 'coping OK with it. I am looking forward to things getting back to normal,' he said, before walking off.

The day wore on, dusk was gathering and the temperature was dropping. Yet there was still no word from the police on what was to happen to Donovan.

'It'll be today lad, it might be late, but it'll happen,' Dave Bruce had assured me. I was prepared to wait. The following day's story was in the bag, so I started to think of ideas for the day after, when the phone rang. Dave was on the other end. 'There's a press conference at 5pm at Dewsbury nick,' he said. 'Donovan's going to be charged with kidnap and false imprisonment.'

CHAPTER 20

POLICE STATION FOYERS ARE INVARIABLY GRIM, DEPRESSING PLACES. It is understandable that parts of stations aren't especially attractive, the cells for one, interview rooms another, but as the police, at least in theory, are public servants, it is surprising that some bright spark up-and-coming copper hasn't hit on the idea of making the station entrances that bit more welcoming. If the police are to operate with the community on their side, making them feel forces are approachable, you'd think that the first point of contact would be somewhere that would put a person at ease, where they might be happy to wait for a while, if necessary. After all, in this consumer-obsessed, business-driven society, are we not all supposed to be customers now?

Those who have ever visited a police station will be familiar with the sights on offer in most entrances: semi-darkness caused by poor quality lighting and a lack of windows; three or four chairs, either with hard seats, or, if cushioned, threadbare to the point they'd give a filthy taxi office armchair a run for its money; a couple of noticeboards, all displaying depressingly familiar crime prevention posters, most of them way out of date, with the notice advising what to do if you find a Colorado Beetle pinned in the corner. It would be interesting to see what happened if someone actually found a Colorado Beetle and bothered to take it down to their local nick. There is also a deserted front counter, with Perspex shutters and a bell that eventually, slowly and grudgingly drags the bored desk constable or civilian worker away from their chat and their brew, only to react to a query with reluctance, at best, or outright rudeness, at worst.

The police station in Dewsbury town centre ticks at least a few of these boxes, and it was here, among the dim lighting and brown-brick flooring that Britain's media gathered, and waited, for the 5pm press conference, to be hosted by the Crown Prosecution Service. That the

CPS, the organisation that reviews evidence brought to it by the police before deciding whether charges can be brought in a case, was to lead the conference, was unusual, at least in my experience. It was said the CPS was trying to improve its public relations and raise its profile, which was why it was appearing before the cameras and notebooks.

The journalists gathered in groups and chatted, the print and broadcast reporters tending to stay with their own, and the foyer was packed. Up to 40 people had squeezed into it, some carrying camera equipment and long-handled microphones, all still wrapped in the extreme weather gear used to keep out the Dewsbury Moor cold. The Daily Mail reporter was, as usual, the exception, still in his usual thin suit. If he was cold, it won't have lasted long, as all the body heat soon sent the temperature skywards.

The clock ticked on and still we were not called in. Every time an internal door opened the pack's eyes turned, its ears picked up, expecting the word that we were to head inside. None came, and word started to arrive, from various sources, that the police and the CPS were unable to agree what charges Donovan should face.

Eventually, just before 6pm, we were told what we had already started to expect: the conference would not now happen before 8pm. Everyone trudged off into the night, muttering to themselves and each other but unable to do anything about it, resigned to a long, late shift. I headed back to the car, parked at Dewsbury Station, from where I phoned through my story about Karen denying the rumours, then, suddenly dog-tired, I reclined the seat and took a cat-nap.

About twenty minutes later I woke up with a jump, cold, stiff and disorientated. I couldn't even remember where I was at first, then it came back. I was in a Dewsbury car park, working, with no clear idea when I was going to see an end to the shift. For the first time during the Shannon story, I felt fed-up, and did not want to be there.

I needed to get moving, to warm up and to eat. A fast-food joint close to the police station, did the trick, so with some kip, junk food and hot tea inside me I was ready to work again. Not exactly leaping into action, but drawing on a grim determination to finish the job.

We all trooped back into the police station. I was glad I'd napped for a few minutes, the other hacks looked noticeably tired now, the chat and black humour still coming but at a slower pace. The Channel 4 cameraman's eyes were bloodshot red, his lids hanging heavy as he chatted with a BBC counterpart. Again, we waited in the foyer, which, in the warmth, now smelt of spices. Several of the reporters had clearly made the best of the wait by sampling one of Dewsbury's fine range of curry houses.

The wait went on, and on, until collective hearts sank when we were told the conference had been postponed again – this time until 9.30pm. Once more, everyone wandered off into the night. Thankfully, the wait seemed shorter this time, and, as the clock crawled towards 9.30, I returned to the police station to find that a copper was at last waiting to guide us out of the foyer and into the beehive of corridors and offices that make up a police station. The drained – and by now slightly tetchy – press people were shown into a small room, which had been set out in classic press conference style, rows of chairs facing a table at the front, two chairs behind it.

The chairs stayed empty for a while longer as the private wrangling must have continued behind the scenes. John Cundy, BBC Look North's long-serving crime correspondent, began to twitch, wondering whether the news would arrive in time for him to make the 10.35pm bulletin. It did. Just. At about 10.10pm, Peter Mann, head of the CPS's Complex Case Unit, walked into the room, followed by an assistant. Despite the long wait, the tiredness in the room and the feeling that we already knew what was coming, there was still a tingle of drama in the air, triggered by the understanding that this was a crucial tipping point in an enormous story.

Mr Mann, a shortish, dark-haired man, looking far from comfortable in the glare of the camera lights, began to read from a prepared statement in a rather quiet, monotone voice. 'In relation to the disappearance and subsequent discovery of Shannon Matthews, the Crown Prosecution Service has been working closely with the police in connection with this case since the arrest of Michael Donovan, also known as Paul Drake, last Friday. As this case has developed, we have been carefully examining and assessing the evidence in order to come to a charging decision at the earliest possible opportunity. Having carefully considered all the material supplied to us by West Yorkshire Police we have made the decision there is sufficient evidence and made the decision that Michael Donovan is charged with kidnapping and false imprisonment.'

That was that. Donovan had been charged and would appear before Dewsbury Magistrates in the morning. No time was allowed for questions, and no journalist appeared to want to ask any, all desperate to write their story then head for home. I took a wrong turning on the way out of the police station and bumped into Mr Mann on some back stairs. Far from being the stiff, unfriendly lawyer I was expecting, he was relaxed and returned my 'Hello' as well as exchanging a few words of small talk. Outside, we went our separate ways into the darkness, both probably thinking that we'd finished with Dewsbury and the strange saga of Shannon Matthews.

CHAPTER 21

WHEN A CRIMINAL who has really managed to get into the heads of the general public arrives at a magistrates court, it is the closest we come in our modern age to the days of the stocks, of public humiliations and even public executions, when the condemned would be paraded before the baying mob, forced to run the gauntlet of the abuse, spittle and missiles, before arriving at the scaffold to meet their grisly end.

These days, the routine is well-rehearsed, and only takes place when someone has been accused of a grave offence, nearly always involving children. A mob gathers early – do they take time off work to do so? Not knowing which security van their target is in, they shout abuse at all of them. It must act as a release, an understandable, if ultimately pointless, way of briefly releasing the intense anger, hatred and frustration they share. Often, though not always, those doing the shouting are from the community that has been hit hardest by the crime. They know that while they will see the accused in the courtroom, the law stops them from venting their spleen there, a law which is generally well respected while a trial is underway. However, volleys of abuse when a judge or magistrate has passed sentence and the hearing is over, are fairly common.

It is a scene repeated countless times in recent years: the man who attacked the van carrying one of the children who murdered James Bulger; the hundreds who turned out to jeer Maxine Carr, girlfriend of double child killer Ian Huntley; and the 200-strong crowd that besieged Chichester Magistrates Court when paedophile and murderer Roy Whiting was remanded in custody.

A separate mob, of photographers, is present for the arrival of the accused, taking pictures of the first mob, then, when the van appears, darting forward to take quick shots of the tiny, blacked out windows at the top of each small compartment in the van, hoping to get lucky and snatch their quarry, the defendant.

The fact Shannon had been found alive, and reportedly unharmed, meant Donovan was treated to a relatively small crowd, although it was a vocal one. Waiting for his custody van to emerge after the short hearing, on Tuesday, March 18, there were shouts of 'scum' and 'give Donovan life' from some Dewsbury Moor residents as he was driven away, back to his Armley prison cell. Twenty police officers had to cordon off the area surrounding the back gate, then lined the cordon themselves to stop anyone trying to break through.

Inside the courtroom, things had been much calmer. Donovan half-shuffled, half-limped into the dock, looking more like a broken man of 75 than one who had yet to turn 40. He stared, with dead, slightly bulging eyes, at the bench as he confirmed his personal details, his own clothes of a blue jumper and grey trousers already resembling prison-issue wear.

In the public gallery were Julie Bushby and Neil and Amanda Hyett, who burst into tears during the five-minute hearing. She later said they were tears of joy, shed with relief that her uncle was not released on bail. Instead, he was remanded in custody, his next appearance arranged to take place through a video link on March 25, the hope being that keeping him at Armley would keep the crowds away from court.

At this point, when someone has been charged and appears in court, the paths of the local and national press often go different ways. Strictly speaking, all media are governed by the same contempt of court rules, in that they are banned from printing anything that might cause substantial risk of serious prejudice to a trial from the moment a case becomes active. In law, that is from arrest, but charges are generally seen as the cut off point. For various reasons though, the national media, mainly the national press, like to push as far as they possibly can at the limits of the law.

There have been times they have got extremely close to the edge, occasionally toppling over it. The Government's top lawyer, the Attorney General, warned the media about its reporting at the beginning of Huntley's case, while lawyers for Rose West, wife of maniac Fred West, attempted to get her case thrown out, claiming she could never get a fair trial. In 2001, a trial in which two Leeds United footballers were among the defendants, and stood accused of viciously assaulting an Asian student, did collapse after an article in the Sunday Mirror was judged to have prejudiced the trial.

By contrast, nearly all local papers, the Yorkshire Evening Post included, plays pretty safe. The hierarchy want to avoid legal costs, the footsoldiers want to avoid the risk of losing their jobs. However that day's YEP front page, the result of the notes Karen and I had exchanged the previous day, was an exclusive headed 'Karen speaks out: We were not involved, despite the rumours.'

In the story, "she" described how hurtful some of the press coverage had been during her three-and-a-half week ordeal, hinting at her involvement, and criticising her and her family, and her home estate. 'At a time when me and my family are under a massive amount of stress, some of the stories have only added to the pain we are all feeling. Please bear this in mind when writing or reporting about a very difficult and personal time in our lives.'

Even though I had written the words, with Karen merely approving them, they sounded authentic and convincing. By this point, I really was starting to suspect all was not right, but, whether through naivety, a desire to believe the best in people, or, more likely, not wanting to believe the worst, I was still giving Karen the benefit of the doubt. But that doubt was now growing, the various strange incidents and bits of erratic behaviour from Karen starting to come together to form strong suspicion in my mind.

There were those early days in the community house, where, the cameras banned, Karen would laugh, smile and joke with people, chatting easily as she shared out or was handed cigarettes. Friend and neighbour Natalie Brown would later describe this in greater detail, saying it seemed Karen led a 'Jekyll and Hyde life,' one persona for the cameras, another in private, the private side seeing her relaxed, laughing, even play-fighting with Craig and Scouse Pete, Natalie's husband. There was the ease with which, on several different occasions, she managed to chomp her way through healthily-sized plates of food, despite the huge, appetite-destroying stress she would have been in, with her daughter missing, the police having no clear leads on how to trace her. And finally, the strangest incident of all, was the time when she leapt from behind her own living room door, tickling my sides and trying to make me jump.

At the end of Donovan's brief day in court there was the first real hint that covering his case would not be as straightforward as it had first appeared. Although neither had been arrested, both Karen and Craig had voluntarily agreed to be questioned by the police. An anonymous "family friend" stressed that the couple were merely helping the police with their ongoing inquiries. 'Karen and Craig knew that they were going to be questioned today,' she said. 'It was all planned. They are doing everything they can to help the police with their investigation.'

CHAPTER 22

KAREN AND CRAIG'S LIVES should have been starting to get back on track. Shannon was safe, the man who appeared to be behind her disappearance was behind bars, awaiting trial, and the press pack camped outside their front door had started to slowly shrink in size. Yet things were far from normal for the pair. Their daughter was still with a foster family, still being slowly, gently, questioned by the police about her time in Craig's uncle's flat. A police community support officer was still stationed outside their front door, seemingly around the clock, and, since their questioning by the police, the whiff of suspicion continuing to hang over them, was growing gradually stronger.

Reflecting this, there were some new, fresher faces in the dwindling gang of press people. At least one national paper was paying freelance photographers to keep watch outside number 24 around the clock, a task I would not have fancied as the temperatures continued to hover close to freezing and dropped below at night.

I asked one young photographer, not long out of college, how he coped with the bitter evenings, and the seemingly endless nights as the clock ticked through the small hours, dawn still an age away, the body at its most vulnerable, prone to falling asleep as its inner-temperature drops. He said that he found sleep almost impossible because of the intense cold, and a powerful cocktail of black coffee and Red Bull kept him wired and awake, his mind racing. 'I keep the engine running to keep warm and do whatever I can to keep my brain occupied. I daredn't read a book though, in case I miss something. I have to keep staring at that dark house. You start to see funny things in front of your eyes in the end.'

The photographer, no doubt glad of some company before starting his shift from hell, chatted to colleagues there with a much easier brief – to witness the planting of "Shannon's tree". The tree, a magnolia, was meant to symbolise a new beginning for Dewsbury Moor after its three weeks of worry. Earlier in the week, Darren Johnson, one of several low-profile stalwarts in the search for Shannon, had dug a bed for the tree and borders for flowers in the front garden of number 24. Darren, whose wife Farrah had also worked endlessly during the search, refused all publicity for his contribution, but was nearly always there, the backbone of the job.

About twenty-five children from Shannon's school had also turned out to help with the planting, while the local vicar, Kathy Robertson, supported by a small group of volunteers, had arrived to lead a service giving thanks for Shannon's rescue. Craig and Karen stood in front of their home, trowels in hand, ready to start gardening, surrounded by Shannon's brothers and sisters. It was a rare public appearance for them since their child was found, the lines of communication having been cut, the support officer still blocking the route to the front door.

The Reverend Robertson had been on the estate before, a calm and reassuring voice for those looking for the schoolgirl, her background and experience bringing a welcome and different dimension to the Search for Shannon campaign. She and her colleagues looked slightly out of place on the Moor, both middle aged and middle class in a mainly young, working class community, but not for one second did they appear uncomfortable or patronising. They were there because they wanted to be there, because they believed in helping their neighbours, no matter who they were or where they were from.

The honour of formally planting the tree went to the eldest Matthews child, with help from his younger siblings. The schoolchildren scurried around, planting the bulbs into the borders with the endearing randomness of a young child playing with a colouring book and crayons. Craig and Karen helped, Karen never smiling once, the two of them seeming to feel awkward and exposed. Behind them, the door to number 24 stood wide open, what little heat there was inside disappearing into the winter night.

As scores of celebratory balloons floated into the heavy grey sky, The Reverend Robertson said the plants were a lasting tribute to the community's commitment to finding its missing member. 'This time, the balloons don't have a message on them,' said Julie Bushby, referring to the regular balloon releases while Shannon was missing, each one of those carrying an appeal for information to help trace her.

The Reverend Robertson, a gentle, bookish-looking woman who speaks with the soft, velvety tones favoured by many clergypeople, praised the Moor's residents for their commitment, for their never-say-die attitude during the long search. 'The people here worked so hard and so well together. The tree is something that will be lasting, while flowers are a sign of hope as they come out each spring. They will show Shannon how much people love her and that they never gave up searching for her; they never gave up hope.'

Surprisingly, Karen also spoke up, saying: 'Thank-you to everyone in the community for everything they have done. We are grateful to all the people from around the country for the time and effort they put in to find Shannon. She is safe and well and that is all that matters.'

The reporters and photographers then hurried away into the gathering gloom, back to their cars and heaters, and the freelance photographer skulked off back to his vehicle, a long night ahead, while Karen closed the door to number 24, and the police community support officer, like the policeman always outside 10 Downing Street, moved back into position. The symbolism was striking. It looked like Karen and Craig were being kept prisoner inside her home, even though the reality was she could come and go as she pleased.

CHAPTER 23

AFTER THE MAGNOLIA TREE had been planted, the contempt of court laws meant the YEP took a step back from the Shannon story, giving me a chance to return, at least briefly, to normal reporting, whatever that may be.

I took a few very welcome days off over the early Easter break, before getting back into the swing of things with a heart-warming story about an ex-miner turned multimillionaire who had decided to donate £10m of his personal fortune to charity. From there followed a tale of a man who had rescued his neighbours from their burning house, a new Leeds band who had got one of their songs onto the Grand Theft Auto soundtrack, and various other pieces from the weird and wonderful world of news.

Yet all the time, in the back of my mind, was Shannon's situation. Questions, more than the obvious ones, still needed to be answered, and before long I wanted to return to the Moor. At the very minimum, I wanted to keep on good terms with my contacts there, ready for the aftermath of Donovan's trial, but by this point, with the whispers and the rumours about Karen and Craig being followed by that out-of-the-blue police questioning, it was starting to look more and more likely that the story was not over.

I drove up there on April Fool's Day, the temperature still chilly but the air fresh, with welcome signs of spring in the air. Walking up the street yet again, the Moor did seem like it had got its life back. The streets were quiet, even deserted, the Shannon posters long gone from the windows, not a single reporter, photographer or cameraman on the streets.

I was there just to say hello, to chat about what had happened and what was yet to come, to keep building upon the trust the Moor's residents had been kind enough to show me. Julie Bushby's was my first stop, the ducks she kept quacking away in the front garden, eyeing me suspiciously but thankfully letting me out in one piece when there was no answer. Julie's dog, Bobby, barked away faintly from the kitchen as I walked off.

Past Scouse Pete's, no one seeming to be at home there either, to Karen and Craig's where, for the first time in weeks, there was no blank face, hidden under a peaked cap, and Day-Glo jacket guarding the door. Their place also seemed to be empty, but I knocked, and, after a short delay, Craig appeared.

There was no invite into the house this time, but I just assumed that the media siege the family had undergone, and some of the coverage they had received, had made them more suspicious.

We chatted on the doorstep, the breeze helping to keep Craig's ever-present B.O. out of my nostrils. He told me that Karen and the kids were away on an outing for the day, giving him the rare luxury of the house to himself. Craig said that family life was beginning to get back to normal, and that he and Karen were relieved to see the press pack had mainly disappeared. 'There's a few here in the mornings, and none on Sundays, that is it now. They aren't gone completely but it is nice to get a bit of a break,' he said.

Craig had a job as a fishmonger at Morrison's supermarket in Heckmondwike, and said he was starting to find his way back to work. 'I've been into work a couple of times, but I'm not back full time yet, Karen needs me here. The other kids are doing okay, but obviously we all want to see Shannon come home.' He also rejected newspaper speculation that Karen was considering suing West Yorkshire Police over her lack of access to Shannon. 'It has not really got anything to do with the police when Shannon comes home.' Craig was more articulate than he was usually given credit for, but that day he did not appear to want to talk. Fair enough, I thought, he must be sick of the press. We shook hands, then I left.

The next morning began in the office as normal, my conversation with Craig filed in my notebook, seemingly nothing more useful than a chat that had helped me keep my eye in on the estate, but at about

As the clock ticks round to 24 hours since Shannon vanished, Chief Superintendent Barry South calls a press conference outside her school. (February 20, 2008)

A very early shot of Craig and Karen, taken on February 27, 2008, the first day they agreed to have their picture taken.

Marching for one of their own: Dewsbury Moor locals turn out in force for a sponsored walk to mark seven days since Shannon vanished. (February 26, 2008)

Lights shine for Shannon: Craig and Karen join friends and neighbours at a candlelit vigil in honour of their missing girl. (March 4, 2008)

A deserted Westmoor Junior School.

Sisterly solidarity: The message on the door into the room Shannon shared with her little sister makes it clear who the space belongs to. (Name obscured for legal reasons).

A little girl's retreat: the YEP was given exclusive access to the Matthews' family home.

Craig shows off
the new bedding
bought ready
'for when
Shannon gets
home.'

The media
village on
Moorside
Road as
family
liaison
officers
Detective
Constable
Christine
Freeman
and
Detective
Constable
Alex
Grummitt
(backs to
camera)
approach
number 24.

Julie Bushby, chairperson of the Moorside Tenants' and Residents' Association, and one of the prime movers in the Search for Shannon campaign.

Karen appears to be feeling the strain. (March 19, 2008)

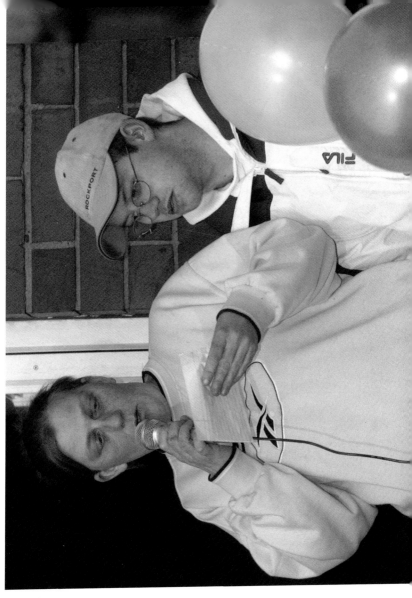

Shannon's welcome home tree has just been planted - and Karen and Craig thank Moor locals for their support. (taken March 19, 2008)

Detective Superintendent Andy Brennan, head of the Shannon inquiry, prepares to speak to the media.

No longer a hiding place: the door to Michael Donovan's flat hangs off its hinges. (March 14, 2008)

The Lidgate
Gardens flats
complex
where
Shannon was
kept prisoner
for 24 days.
(March 14,
2008)

9.30am, news editor Gillian Haworth came up to my desk with her serious face on. It was clear something was breaking. 'Richard, how old is Craig?' she said.

'He's 22.'

Gillian then told me what was going on. Just a few minutes earlier, West Yorkshire Police had confirmed that a 22-year-old man from the Dewsbury Moor area had been arrested on suspicion of possessing indecent images of children. It had to be Craig, and I had to move quickly to confirm the story for that day's paper. At that time the YEP ran several editions, but the final deadline was 1pm; I didn't have much time to spare.

Dave Bruce handled things from the office while I headed for the Moor. By the time I got there, Dave's police contacts had confirmed that Craig was the man under arrest. Dewsbury Moor had comfortably absorbed, even embraced, the media storm that erupted the weekend Shannon was found. After all, it was the story they had all been praying and working for, and understandably they were happy to be within the eye of it. Compared to that, the events unfolding now were like an earthquake erupting underneath the Moor, shockwaves rippling into all the estate's homes and beyond. To many people's astonishment, Craig was now under arrest, and the charges he faced would leave them undecided over whose alleged crimes - Mick Donovan or Craig Meehan - appalled them the most.

The press pack was back, and in a big way and the uniforms had returned to the door of number 24 as well, two of them this time, as CID and forensic officers worked away inside.

My job now was to set the scene from Moorside Road – and then find Karen. One place I knew she definitely wasn't was with Shannon. Dave also told me that April 2 was meant to be the date of Shannon's second meeting with her mother, but that the rendezvous had been cancelled because of Craig's arrest. It being the Easter holidays, Karen and the kids were out for the day again, Julie and her Residents' Association colleagues working especially hard, as they always did, to keep the young ones occupied while the schools were shut. The question was, where had they gone? It didn't take long to find out. The trip was a few miles away, at Oakwell Hall, in Birstall. It was where I needed to be as well.

Just before setting off, I asked a couple of neighbours their thoughts about Craig's arrest – and the allegations against him. One near-neighbour, who asked not to be named, said he had been told that police had found images on Craig's computer some time ago, but added, 'There are that many people use that computer, not just Craig.' He said that he would wait to hear the facts before reaching any conclusions on today's developments, but added an ominous rider to that. 'I can't speak for everyone on this estate, some people like to act first and ask the questions later or not at all. It could be difficult for him to come back here.'

A couple of other reporters arrived at Oakwell at about the same time as I did. The trip was easy to spot, about 20 children and half-a-dozen women from the Residents' Association, picnicking in one of the fields. They seemed underdressed for the cold weather, most in short sleeves and flimsy, pump-type shoes without socks. The kids had thin coats on, but that lack of warmth was neutralised by the fact they were running around, enjoying the open air as children do.

I felt awkward approaching them. This was a rare awayday for those youngsters, and what was going on with Craig and Karen had nothing to do with them. Asking questions of the women with them felt like an intrusion, but, Julie being Julie, I needn't have worried. From start to finish, she had given the impression she had seen it all before, and she grinned as I walked over, chewing on a piece of gum. 'She's not here. And I can't tell you where she is,' Julie said. I didn't want to press the issue, especially given the subject matter and the young ears listening, so we chatted quietly for no more than a minute or two.

Like most people who had been closest to Karen, Julie was prepared to let the legal system do its work. 'It makes me feel sick to think he might have done it. But you are innocent until proven guilty,' she said. But her next comment was about Shannon. 'I don't think Shannon will be coming home now. I'm assuming social services will have to get involved and take the other three kids away until it is all sorted out, whenever that is.'

CHAPTER 24

CRAIG WAS CHARGED WITHIN 24 HOURS OF BEING ARRESTED, stopping the media merry-go-round back at Dewsbury Magistrates Court. The hearing briefly took the media gaze away from Karen, and she was able to get to the postponed meeting with her daughter, at a secret location, where mother and child spent more than three hours together.

Meanwhile Craig was brought into the Dewsbury dock wearing a black Manchester United away shirt, with Cristiano Ronaldo's name on the back. 'I wonder how his Man Utd shirt went down when they took him into Armley,' a person in the public gallery half-whispered. Armley is Leeds's prison, and a deep, historic hatred festers between Leeds United and Manchester United fans. There would be many of the former in Armley, both prisoners and prison officers.

The court heard how police searching for Shannon had seized the two computers at number 24, one Craig's, the other Karen's, to search for clues about where the missing girl might be. The hope was she might have left hints through emails, or social networking sites. Instead, police found about 140 child porn images, some of them rated at level four, for their seriousness. The worst images are rated level five.

Throughout the hearing, Craig sat with a blank look on his face, surrounded by three burly guards, but what would normally have been a five-minute hearing doubled in length, as Craig's solicitor, Robert Dawson, explained why he would not be applying for bail. Compared to other cases involving indecent images, the number of images on Craig's computer was small, and I had seen defendants with many more stored on their machines get bail. However, Mr Dawson said: 'Mr Meehan should remain in custody for his own protection and safety. In normal circumstances I would be making a bail application and it wouldn't be opposed. The difference here is because of the publicity surrounding this case. The address that he has is not suitable to be put forward for the court. I cannot put forward a suitable address so he cannot make a bail application.'

Those few, short sentences, were an acknowledgement that Craig's life could now never be the same again. While many of his neighbours on the Moor were prepared to wait and see justice done, there would be many more, both in Dewsbury and beyond, who would not be so patient with someone accused of child sex offences. For about a month, Craig's face had been in the media nearly every day. Instantly recognisable, and an easy target, his legal team believed he would be better off in jail.

At first, it was an opinion Craig appeared not to share. Stories emerged that he believed he would be able to return to the Moor safely, and suggested an address, around the corner from Moorside Road, where he claimed to have been offered a room. He followed this up with a number of bail applications, some heard in private by a Crown Court judge, but all were refused, while Craig himself rejected an offer of bail to a hostel outside of the Dewsbury area. Family members claimed he did this because it was easier for him to stay in touch with them from prison, rather than a hostel.

When Craig woke up the following day in his Armley cell, he would read newspaper stories of how he had been dumped by Karen. Despite the whispering campaign against her, public sympathy was firmly with her about Craig, and friends told the YEP that she had asked them to clear her ex-partner's things out of number 24.

Karen's best friend, Petra Jamieson, said, 'Karen has said she no longer wants to be part of Craig's life. She hasn't told him face-to-face but I think he'll assume that after what's gone on. I can't begin to imagine what's going on in Karen's head.'

Julie Bushby added: 'She woke up on Wednesday morning excited about seeing Shannon but then her whole world collapsed. She is horrified about what's happened and cannot get over it. It's over between them. She's so confused, her life is in turmoil.' Julie also revealed more about the time Karen had spent with her daughter. 'She gave her a cuddle, played in a sandpit, talked and painted pictures with her daughter. It was a very emotional time for them both. They had a wonderful time.'

Other arrests were made that week, though the suspects were bailed and eventually released without charge. The Moor, which had been getting back on track, was now in a state of turmoil that locals felt was even worse than when Shannon was missing. At that point, they were all together, banded as one in their determination to bring the girl home. With these arrests, neighbours were inevitably looking at neighbours, wondering who would be next and what exactly had been going on.

Petra admitted as much, saying the arrests had shaken the community. 'Before Wednesday we seemed to get back to a bit of normality. There was no press and then on Wednesday morning I got a phone call and came outside and thought "what's happened?" It's been more confusing than anything else, it's still not sinking in for many of us. One minute we're on a high then next minute we're brought right back down.'

Amanda Hyett must have felt especially lost, as her husband, Neil, in his job as a coach driver, was away working in Spain at the time. Around the same time, the two became the first – and only – Moor residents to appoint a media representative. Even at what had again become a very strange time, it seemed a highly unusual thing to do. But there was no time to dwell on it as events took yet another momentous turn.

CHAPTER 25

THE POLICE CAME FOR KAREN LAST OF ALL, and, in the end, the pressure had become so unbearable, she willingly handed herself to them. Over that previous week, as she had first seen the man she had shared her life with for four years arrested on child sex abuse charges, then the people closest to him picked up, Karen must have started to wonder if, or more likely when, her own turn was coming.

On the evening of Sunday, April 5, two of the women closest to Karen used some classic Yorkshire bluntness to drag the truth from her. Julie Bushby and Natalie Brown, wife of Scouse Pete, confronted Karen with their suspicions. Both women had spotted what they thought were inconsistencies in Karen's story, and Natalie, who, like Julie, is not one for suffering fools gladly, accused her of lying and asked her former friend if she had known where Shannon was all along.

The two women asked for a meeting at a neutral, private place, and Karen was driven there by Detective Constable Christine Freeman, one of two family liaison officers who had been at Karen's side for much of the time Shannon was away. Arriving at the meeting place, Natalie and Julie got into the back of the car, Karen in the front. Natalie, confronting Karen about the growing rumours on the estate that she had been involved, accused her of lying and asked her former friend if she had known where Shannon was all along.

Karen nodded, replied 'Yes,' then started to sob, cry and shake. She said that as the search for Shannon went on, the hours turning into days and then weeks, that she felt everything got out of control and she was unable to stop it, shame stopping her from telling the truth. After hearing what Karen had to say, Detective Constable Freeman arrested her on the spot on suspicion of perverting the course of justice. Karen was handcuffed and first taken to Dewsbury police station, where she was held overnight, before being transferred to Wakefield the following afternoon.

The news broke to the press late on Sunday, West Yorkshire Police releasing a statement at about 11.30pm that night which said a 32-year-old woman from Dewsbury Moor had been arrested on suspicion of perverting the course of justice. Like Donovan, she was quizzed for hours, detectives having to apply for more time to hold her without charge and continue their questioning. Confusion reigned among the press as to exactly where Karen was being held. I headed for Dewsbury Police Station on the Monday morning, although my usefulness there was limited. I wouldn't exactly be able to interview Karen, so my work would be limited to a line or two, reporting what happened if she emerged, or in the unlikely event the mob turned out to the station. They usually saved themselves for the magistrates' courts.

Staking out the police station was mainly a job for the photographers, and they were out in force. Occasions such as that one, which involve long periods of hanging about, often in the cold, but having to keep the attention switched on to full so as not to miss the shot, are when the lensmen and women really earn their money. Between 15 and 20 photographers, from various local and national papers, news agencies and the self-employed freelances, were on a piece of pavement at the back of the police station, from which the back door could be seen. General agreement was that Karen would not be brought out through the front, but had the police wanted to get her out unseen that would have been the best way, as not a single journalist was keeping an eye on the main entrance.

YEP photographer Jonathan Gawthorpe was there with me, as we waited, waited and waited. Once more I kept pondering Karen's behaviour, the things I had seen her do when she was away from the full glare of the cameras. With the benefit of hindsight, things started to fall into place, her behaviour starting to make sense. There were the times in number 24 and in the community house, when she seemed relaxed, able to chat and seemingly take her mind off the fact her eldest daughter had gone, leaving no clues, as though she had been abducted by aliens. All the food she had managed to put away, meals I had explained away as comfort eating, and then the staggering moment when she leapt out at me from behind her living room door.

All these things had struck me as slightly strange at the time, but almost as soon as those thoughts entered my head I pushed them to the back of my mind and moved on. Firstly, I told myself, who was I to say how a person suffering unimaginable trauma must be feeling - how could I possibly know? Second I had to keep an open mind, and, at first just listen and take what I am being told in good faith. On some stories, claims can be checked the same day, "the other side" contacted for their take on it; on others, it is a simple case of checking the facts against what you have been told. On the Shannon story, we were playing a long game, there to help a community bring a missing child back. As I was concentrating on that job, not wanting to believe the worst in people, I had listened to the rumours, mentally gathered the oddments of evidence, but kept an open mind as long as possible until those dark, dark rumours began to rise irresistibly to the surface.

We continued to stand on the cold tarmac. The job became an endurance test for the photographers: who could last the longest without going to the toilet, which was a couple of minutes' walk away in Dewsbury Bus Station. All had been drinking tea and coffee, all were cold, but all were desperate to get that killer shot of Karen in handcuffs. Hunger started to hit as well, and the local Gregg's had a field day when I walked in, armed with an order from more than a dozen cold and hungry journalists. People walked past, most of them commenting in some way either on the Shannon affair or our presence on the streets. A grimy teenager with black bum-fluff under his nose, 18 or 19 years old, tracksuit bottoms tucked firmly into socks shouted 'scum' at us, an insult most journalists have heard so often it long ago stopped having an effect, and now raises only a smile. I'm not sure he knew why we were there, and was more likely showing off to his girlfriend. From the look of the vacant expression underneath a pile of badly-dyed blonde hair, it seemed he was wasting his time, as all her concentration looked like it was going on stopping her from toppling over on the huge wedge-like shoes she was wearing.

As is usually the case, most people either totally ignored us, in that classically British way, whatever was going on being none of their business, or were genuinely interested in what was happening and politely asked us. People tutted in the general direction of the police station when we told them why we were there, some of the more sympathetic comments saying what a disgrace it all was, others indulging in a bit of good old summary justice, calling for Karen to be strung up.

There were various flurries of excitement amongst the waiting pack as unmarked cars came and went, particularly when they sped into the car park and stopped near the back door, but none of them had anything to do with Karen, as far as we could make out. Then, some of the main detectives from the case turned up, walked into the station and were not seen again all day. Eventually, the police took pity on us, a friendly constable being sent out to tell us that Karen definitely was not in the building. Those who had been crossing their legs sighed loudly with relief at that point before dashing off down the hill.

By this time, various unconfirmed stories had begun to leak out to the press. One was, as we all expected, that both Karen and Mick were blaming each other for what happened, Karen claiming that Mick was the abductor he had at one point appeared to be, Mick accusing Karen of manipulating him and planning the whole sorry saga. Police sources had already told some reporters that in his interviews, Donovan had been claiming that other Matthews family members had known where Shannon was.

Two theories emerged as to why Karen would conspire with Mick. The first was that she had been planning to leave Craig, and had packed her bags ready to go back on that late February day. As that strange source in the blacked-out 4x4 had claimed, Donovan had taken a shine to Shannon after meeting her at a family event, thought to be the funeral of Craig Meehan's father, and so was happy to take her in and give Karen a place to stay while she found her feet. There were also claims, one of them from Donovan's niece, Amanda Hyett, appearing in a Sunday newspaper, that he and Karen had been having an affair and had planned to start a new life together.

One Moorside Road resident, close to Karen, said: 'She was going to leave Craig, she had her bags of clothes packed. But she bottled it at the last second. Craig started asking where Shannon was, and she couldn't exactly say she was with Mick Donovan. So she pretended she thought Shannon was with Craig, then in the end she had to report her missing. It ended up getting way out of control after that.'

The second theory doing the rounds was that the whole affair was cooked up by Karen and various family members in the hope of conning some money, either from the McCann family's fund, or in a half-baked attempt to copy an episode of the Channel 4 series "Shameless". That episode, broadcast just a month before Shannon vanished, saw one of the main characters, Debbie Gallagher, stage the kidnapping of little brother Liam to help her waster of a dad, Frank, out of a financial hole when he falsely claimed to have won a fortune on The Lottery. Bizarre though it sounded, the theory was taken so seriously by police that the Shannon inquiry team asked Channel 4 for a copy of the tape.

No longer needed at the police station – it turned out Karen was still at Wakefield - I headed for the Moor. Unsurprisingly, the mood there was confused and downbeat, although what was surprising was the refusal of many to jump to an immediate condemnation of Karen. There was plenty of anger going her way, but mostly people just wanted to know what had happened and why. This was refreshing, because so often as a reporter you can write the story even before you've got there, people's reactions predictable, especially if they are angry or grieving. It was another example of the Moor confounding popular expectations. Despite all the stress and worry, and the effort that Karen's neighbours had put in for her, only to end up feeling betrayed, not one was calling for harsh, quick-fix justice. The contrast was huge with those passers-by near the police station, who were often calling for a woman they did not know, had never met and who was innocent until proven guilty, to be executed.

Craig and Karen's house was empty, with both of them in custody and the children with neighbours, but two police support officers were now on guard outside the front door. The oldest child was due to celebrate his twelfth birthday in two days' time.

When I saw Pete Brown, he said everyone who had been involved had been left feeling hollow. 'You can't help but feel down. Everyone worked their socks off, so it's really upsetting to hear this, you feel hurt. This estate pulled together and I'm worried the atmosphere will change now. We are all wondering what the truth is, it has gone on so long and the community is tired, now there will be all this extra pressure on it. We keep getting rid of the papers, then something else happens and they are all back again. You wonder what will happen next, when this will end.'

Petra Jamieson had taken in at least one of her best friend Karen's children while she was at the police station. She said: 'We all want to know what has happened. But whatever it is, she will still be my friend and I will still support her 100 per cent. When I see her though, I will definitely be asking her why.'

If some reports are accurate, Karen came close to facing charges alone. On the evening of Saturday, April 5, prison officers sounded the alarm when they spotted Donovan collapsed in his cell, lying there in a pool of his own blood. He had slit his wrists, and was rushed to Leeds General Infirmary. He was treated there overnight and returned to prison the following day. Just how bad his injuries were is unclear. The prison service described the cuts as 'a serious attempt at self harm,' but one of Dave Bruce's police sources was dismissive, telling him: 'I have cut myself worse while shaving.'

Serious or not, Donovan survived and within a few hours, the woman he had met through his estranged nephew would be standing alongside him in the dock.

CHAPTER 26

ON WEDNESDAY, APRIL 9, three days after she was arrested, Karen Matthews stood in the same Dewsbury Magistrates Court dock that Craig Meehan and Mick Donovan had occupied before her. As with Donovan, the person who told the world of the charges against her was Peter Mann, head of the Crown Prosecution Service's Complex Case Unit. At a press conference, the day before the court appearance, Mr Mann said: 'Having carefully considered all of the evidence provided in the file by West Yorkshire Police, we have decided that there is sufficient evidence and have authorised that Karen Matthews be charged with perverting the course of justice and child neglect. She is in the process of being charged and will appear before Dewsbury Magistrates Court on Wednesday morning. We will continue to keep this case under constant review.'

Karen was led into the courtroom in handcuffs, the shackles released as she took her place in the dock. So many people had turned up to see the short hearing, there was not enough space in the courtroom to fit them all in. Senior detectives from the Shannon inquiry were there, as were the two main family liaison officers, one of whom had listened to Karen crumble and confess.

Her complexion was normally pale, not unusual for someone with red hair, but on this morning her face looked a sickly yellow-white, with puffy red rings around her eyes, the face of someone who had not slept or eaten properly for some time. It was a picture of strain the nation had seen before, but one that had dropped away in private moments. This time, the pain and pressure were real. An entire nation was once again looking at this woman, but now the gaze had changed from one of immense sympathy to one of confusion, at best. At worst, it was one of fury and outright revulsion.

At this point Karen was facing charges of perverting the course of justice, by repeatedly lying to the police, and child neglect.

Looking shamed, she turned to the familiar faces in the public gallery, her eyes pleading with them, and shook her head. Her solicitor, Roger Clapham, told the Bench his client denied having any knowledge of where Shannon was during the twenty-four day search and applied for his client to be released on bail so she could stay in contact with her children, giving the court a relative's address outside the Dewsbury area. As with Craig's bail application, the plea was thrown out on the grounds that the risk to Karen's safety would be too great should she be freed.

It was at this point that Karen's friends and neighbours, those who had stood side-by-side while her daughter was away, showed their first clear anti-Karen feelings. As the bail application was thrown out, some, though not all, shouted 'Yes!'

Outside the court, in a touching show of solidarity, those friends and neighbours stood in a line, hand-in-hand, as if acting out the way they had behaved, the solidarity they had shown, while they believed they were searching for a missing girl. The line included Pete and Natalie Brown, Neil and Amanda Hyett, Caroline Meehan, Petra Jamieson and Julie Bushby. It was done off-the-cuff, but was a powerful way for those good people to show the world's media they were proud of what they had done. They had acted in good faith, and, if the same situation arose, they would do it all again. Reporting restrictions meant few of their views or opinions could be printed or broadcast, but that simple, dignified demonstration meant that no words were needed. Pictures of the line-up were broadcast on the TV news and printed in several national newspapers.

As with Donovan, police officers lined up to form a cordon as Karen was driven away to begin life in her temporary home, New Hall Prison, in Wakefield. The now infamous 24 Moorside Road was to enter a state of limbo, as shortly after the remand hearing, Kirklees Council workers arrived to fit metal shutters over its doors and windows. At that point, Karen was still an innocent woman, and so the council had to keep her home available for her should she be found not guilty. The authority also had to bear in mind the risk of local hotheads taking out their anger on an easy target like her house. A quick-thinking neighbour had already moved and re-planted Shannon's magnolia tree, put into the ground at that touching ceremony just a few weeks earlier.

The fear that anger was starting to boil over was clearly growing, as Dewsbury Moor beat officers decided to hold clear-the-air talks with the estate's residents. Officers also took the unusual step of printing and distributing leaflets, urging locals to stay calm and let the police get on with their job. It read: 'We realise that people may be confused about recent events. We cannot go into detail about our investigation, but we would like to reassure you that we will find out the truth. It is important that the community does not jump to any conclusions about people who may be involved in this inquiry. Please do not take the law into your own hands and leave police to do their job.' The leaflet also thanked residents for their 'help and support' in the weeks since Shannon was reported missing.

The police's far-sighted efforts to stave off trouble seemed to do the trick, with no serious incidents reported on the Moor in the days following Karen's court appearance, while number 24 also escaped any attempts to burn it down. Again, a community which had absorbed huge pressure, of many different kinds, did itself proud, coming through an extremely tense time with dignity, its collective head held deservedly high.

CHAPTER 27

IT WAS AS IF THEY HAD SWAPPED PLACES IN THE DOCK. A couple of days after his former partner had faced the Dewsbury Bench, Craig stood in the same spot to answer his child porn charges. By then, the backlash against Karen was well and truly underway, the abuse being channeled towards her, fuelled by a string of tabloid stories, arguably worse than that which was being sent in Craig's direction.

The tabloid press loves a national hate figure. Reflecting the views of much of its readership, there is little room for reason or explanation as to why someone may have done something, no space to bring in background or comparison. Guilty seems to mean something more than guilty, as if the punishment is not just that which the court hands down but must include a public flogging through the pages of a newspaper. The tabloids love it all the more if the offender is a woman. A man will do, but the traditional stereotypes about "the fairer sex" make it all the easier to turn a woman into a figure of hate, and since Myra Hindley died, the title "most evil woman in the land" had been vacant. An attempt to promote Maxine Carr to that position ran out of steam. Now Karen seemed to have been placed on a fast track to public enemy number one status.

If someone is guilty they rightly have to take and serve the sentence handed down by the court, but for some people, the sentence does not seem to be enough, and as a nation we delight in hauling people over the coals and back again, in an ultimately futile attempt to ease some of the anger we feel at whoever has been placed in the stocks.

Behind bars in New Hall Prison, Karen was shielded from it a little. Her friends were not. Petra, who had not flinched from her promise to stand by Karen, told the YEP that she had been abused in the street by strangers following her pal's arrest. Petra also said that because she was a potential witness, she had been unable to visit Karen in jail, and, at that time, thought that no one, not even any family members, had been to see her. 'I am being treated as a witness and so I can't speak to her, although I am allowed to write to her as long as I don't mention the case. I am going to write her a letter because I hope it will give her a real boost. I am going to stand by her, it doesn't mean I don't have the same questions everyone else does, but what sort of friend would I be if I abandoned her now? It was horrible to be abused like that but I am just trying to get on with it and I'm still not going to jump to any conclusions.'

Meanwhile, the tabloids were having a field day. One claimed Karen had been placed on suicide watch amid fears for her safety in prison and said that she was in fear of her life after fellow inmates had told her 'it was only a matter of time' before they got to her, having placed a bounty of ten cigarettes on her head. It also said Karen was spending 20 hours a day alone in her single cell writing letters - up to four A4 pages covered in misspellings and crossings out - to Shannon.

About a month later, claims a tobacco bounty had been placed on Craig's head were printed in another tabloid. The stories were almost identical, one of the few differences being the names. Even more far-fetched stories were not hard to find. A Sunday tabloid claimed that Karen had been given a personal food tester in jail, after inmates threatened to poison her meals with bleach, glass and rat-killer, and that she was being treated 'like royalty', with a gang of guards protecting her whenever she left her cell. The same paper also said that Karen had gone on hunger strike, and stoked up anger by reporting she was in line for a new identity – like "evil" Maxine Carr – when released from prison.

A daily paper story used quotes claiming Dewsbury Moor was 'worse than Beirut' and a real-life version of Channel 4's "Shameless". Some of the stories carried direct quotes, some of them did not, but few had the words of those once closest to Karen and

Craig. They had enough on their plates. The night before Craig appeared in court, about sixty of the Moor's residents had attended a meeting at Shannon's school, Westmoor, held as part of the police's efforts to keep the estate calm.

Some of the people there spoke up angrily about the way some parts of the media had portrayed Dewsbury Moor. But Chief Superintendent Barry South told the residents: 'We are proud of you and nothing's going to change that.' And he urged them to stick together throughout the months to come. 'Whatever the outcome, whatever the anger, whatever your feelings are, for goodness sake, put them to one side. If I said to you on day one we will find Shannon but this is going to happen, you would have had that. For those of you who are thinking "right we are not happy with this", it's done; that little girl is back with us.'

The efforts worked, an uneasy calm held, and Craig's court appearance, while held before a packed room, passed off quietly and peacefully. Despite that, magistrates rejected Craig's claim, made through his barrister, David Orbaum, that he could be bailed safely back to the Moor, and he was remanded in custody for his own safety. This time there was no gang waiting to shout their anger at the van as he was taken back to jail. Understandably, the Moor's residents were weary, wanting to get on with their lives. Now the story had moved from their doorsteps to the courtrooms, they might get the chance to start doing that.

CHAPTER 28

NINE DAYS AFTER SHE WAS ARRESTED, Karen Matthews' path in life was again firmly entwined with Mick Donovan's. This time though, she did not have any say in it, the legal system fixing a date for the pair to stand trial together, though the two would not have to stand alongside each other in the dock as to avoid the problems involved in moving Karen, it was arranged that she would appear at Leeds Crown Court through a videolink from New Hall Prison.

Her face, when it flickered into sight on the screen, made a strange image. Filming or photography are absolutely forbidden in a courtroom, such a serious contempt of court that anyone attempting it could be jailed on the spot, so it is always unusual when any footage is shown in court, even if it is for evidence. When defendants appear via videolink, even though the link-up is always quite short, it is as if the frowned-upon medium of television is making its first push into one of the last areas of our TV-drenched society to have resisted it. Karen stared straight into the camera, her face expressionless, the emotion that had been etched into it now missing, replaced by a pale, impassive mask

At that April hearing, it was agreed that Karen and Mick would go before a judge together for the first time on July 11, when they would enter their pleas. Their provisional trial date was set for November 11, Armistice Day, and the possibility of moving it out of the Dewsbury area was discussed. Newcastle Crown Court, which has hosted high profile Leeds area trials before, was mentioned as an option. Lawyers were concerned that all the publicity surrounding the case might affect the judgement of a locally-selected jury, concerns that led to cases such as that of David Bieber, the American bodybuilder who murdered a policeman in Leeds, being switched to the North-East. The concerns that sensational media coverage might put the trial at risk, or prejudice it, was so strong that lawyers at that hearing appealed to the media to be restrained in their reporting.

A couple of days after Karen's video appearance, there was a development that we had to report. The three main players from the Shannon saga – Karen, Craig and Mick – were all taken from their respective prison cells by detectives working on the case and questioned at length over a seven-hour session. The step was unusual in that Karen and Mick had already appeared in court to face charges over the Shannon case. Craig had not, though he was arrested and bailed inside the prison system in connection with Shannon's disappearance, but was never charged with any offence linked to his former step-daughter's time away from home.

The reason for those lengthy interviews became clear when Karen and Mick at last made their way into the dock together, at a plea hearing delayed from July until early September. Co-defendants are brought into court handcuffed to a security guard, and, while they are held in separate cells they may see each other on the stairs on the way up the dock. This must make for some awkward moments for defendants who are not on good terms, not least because they must go through the same routine, into and out of the dock, several times a day during the trial, when they must also sit close together in a confined space for day after day.

When Karen and Mick were brought into court, any doubt about their contempt for each other, or at least Karen's contempt towards Mick, disappeared. She was brought in first, her face set into a snarl of anger as she was released from the handcuffs, sitting firmly down into the seat and folding her arms, like a sullen teenager forced by her parents to go to a dull aunt and uncle's home.

She was heavily made up, had tried to dress smartly in a beige jacket, buttoned up to the neck, and appeared to have put on a weight while inside. One former neighbour took the make-up as evidence Karen had been assaulted in prison. 'She never wears make-up. It's to cover the bruises,' she said. 'The weight must come from sitting in her cell all day, she's scared to go out there's that many people after her.'

Mick came in second, the two not even glancing in each other's direction. In contrast to Karen, who clearly understood what was going on, even if her face did not always reveal what she made of it all, her co-defendant did not appear altogether clear what was happening or why he was there. Still dressed in his prison gear of blue sweatshirt and grey trousers, he looked gaunt, pale and drawn, with bags under his protruding eyes. Throughout the hearing he appeared distracted, his gaze flitting around the courtroom.

Parts of trials can be intensely boring, but the key moments can bring drama of the highest sort. As Karen and Mick stood to have the charges read to them, the atmosphere in court, although completely silent, was crackling. Surprisingly, few members of the public had made it to that hearing, perhaps because of the rearranged date, yet the demand from the media had been so high the court had had to give out tickets for a seat on the press benches.

Those in the court heard immediate confirmation that the police believed Karen had been involved in Shannon's abduction from the very start; she and Mick were jointly charged with kidnapping Shannon and then falsely imprisoning her. The charges of perverting the course of justice also still stood against the pair.

Karen entered her plea: 'Not Guilty!' in a loud, clear voice, but Mick's tones were barely audible, seemingly straining even to be heard in the deafening silence. Legal matters were discussed, then, forty-five minutes after being brought into court, the two defendants were taken back down to their cells.

CHAPTER 29

AS THE CASE AGAINST SHANNON'S ALLEGED KIDNAPPERS made its slow progress through the court system, it brought a bit of respite to Dewsbury Moor. Gradually, the stories about the two defendants started to decrease, and became slightly less hysterical, although the tabloids still reported with relish that, at the age of 32, Karen had been employed in the first job she had ever held in her life while on remand in prison. The job was prison work, paying a few pounds a week.

The respite from the media allowed the Moor to return to normality, the Residents' Association leading a string of events for the local kids over the school holidays, with the whole community turning out for the annual gala in August. A few days later, the focus shifted to Craig, almost the forgotten man, as he went on trial – the press pack and his former friends and neighbours there to witness it.

Some offences are automatically dealt with by magistrates' courts, others automatically by the crown court, while in some, the defendant can choose in which court they want to appear. Criminals often choose the crown court, deciding they would prefer to take a chance on a jury than three volunteers drawn from the local community: 'trial by Rotary Club' and 'trial by do-gooders' are just two of the slightly unfair comments I have heard made about the magistrates' court system. Craig had taken the slightly surprising step of choosing to be tried by the magistrates' court, with Dewsbury the venue; it was in Dewsbury that the alleged offences had been committed and, by tradition, justice is done locally.

However Craig's case would not be tried by the traditional three-handed magistrates' court bench, but by a district judge, Jonathan Bennett. District judges, who replaced the old stipendiary magistrates, are not volunteers, but paid, and are generally no-nonsense, ultra-businesslike figures. So it was with DJ Bennett. A cross between

Elton John and Richard Whiteley in appearance, he was a man who clearly had a sense of humour, managing to smile from time to time throughout the long hearing while keeping an iron grip on it at all times.

The media pack, including reporters from almost every national newspaper and half-a-dozen local papers, the BBC, both local and national, ITN, Sky and several radio reporters, and a big group of Moor locals and pressmen, filled the benches of the court room, mingling easily with each other now, many on first name terms as they shared a joke. Neil and Amanda Hyett were there and Peter and Natalie Brown, Julie Bushby and, from time to time, her daughter Tiffany, Saleem Khan and Caroline Meehan, older sister of Craig and Amanda, put in a couple of appearances. Alice Meehan, Craig's mother, briefly called in and Leon Rose, Shannon's natural father, was also there. A man who seems to be quiet by nature, he declined to comment to reporters and pretty much kept to himself, chatting occasionally with Karen's former friends.

On top of all those, the public seating included a couple of people who were not from the Moor or the media but ordinary members of the public. One of them, a man wearing a beard and sandals, sat motionless through the entire case, listening to every word. The other, a woman with long blonde hair, said she regularly visits courts in Yorkshire when an interesting case came up. She was armed with a clipboard and paper, and, as far as I could see, never stopped writing while she was in there, recording every word said. When I asked her why she did this, she said it was purely out of personal interest.

All those bodies packed the courtroom and public gallery, with just about every seat full. DJ Bennett barely glanced towards the public seats, concentrating on what was going on with the lawyers and the defendant, or, for the first hour of the first day, was not going on. Delays are as much of a fixture of the British legal system as those strange wigs that judges and barristers insist on wearing in crown court, and delays caused by either prison vans getting stuck in traffic or lawyers needing more time are something even the strictest judge can do nothing about. Both problems surfaced throughout Craig's five-day trial, and, at 10am on the first day, the case was not ready to start. As the delay was announced, there was a brief moment of drama, as it was mentioned that Karen might be called as a witness. Sadly for the media, but happily for court security staff, her evidence was not needed.

Things moved slowly when the court case finally got under way. Every piece of evidence, whether a fragment, a nugget or a gold bar, had to be presented and examined, the prosecution making its case, the defence challenging it. The judge was expected to keep track of everything that was said, and evaluate it thoroughly before pronouncing his verdict, a daunting task in any case, but particularly so in one that might include highly technical evidence.

During a long hearing, in a warm room, as gentle voices burr away in the background, I have sometimes felt my eyes starting to droop, and have seen elderly judges and the odd juror start to go too. I have heard that some judges keep smelling salts in their robes if they need an ultra-quick wake up. For the most part though, I am impressed by how well those in charge keep a grip on a case, piping up after over an hour of silence to query a seemingly minor point. DJ Bennett never once looked like he was flagging, and made seemingly obscure queries several times, including asking where one of Craig's computers was in relation to the door into the Matthews/Meehan living room.

Such questions are designed to give as full a picture as possible of the case being heard. A court reporter gets the full picture too, but must then squeeze a full day's hearing into a 350 word report, or a two minute television or radio broadcast. These space and time restrictions mean the reporter must pick the most interesting point from the day and build the report around that, acting as the public's eyes and ears in court, a tradition that can be traced back hundreds of years to when justice really was done in public, in the square in front of the whole village.

Craig's village, of course, was there to see him face justice, and, about an hour later than the scheduled start time, they saw their man led into court, still wearing the black Manchester United away shirt he had on at his first appearance, way back in April. The stench of B.O., bad at the best of the times, must have been eye-watering.

Prosecuting counsel, David Holderness, outlined his case to the court. He told how the Shannon inquiry team had taken the computer as part of their investigation, but, when checking its hard drive, had found 133 indecent images of children on it, with one further image on Craig's phone. Mr Holderness said that when examining the computer, detectives found search words including 'rape', 'incest' and 'daughter' had been used. He also said that records from Craig's employers, Morrison's in Heckmondwike, showed that all but one of the images had been downloaded at times when he was not at work. Mr Holderness added that the password 'Reggie07' had been used to protect the computer. Reggie was Craig's nickname, widely used by people on the Moor while the search for Shannon went on. Perhaps most damaging for Craig, was the assertion that he had denied using any sort of pornography, yet police had then found a stash of adult videos and DVDs when they raided 24 Moorside Road. If the prosecution could prove that, it demonstrated that Craig was not only a user of pornography but a liar as well

The first "smelling salts session" came that afternoon, as Detective Constable Andrew James, of West Yorkshire Police's Hi-Tech Crime Unit, went into important but dull detail about the background of Craig's second-hand computer and how the images may have come to be on it. DJ Bennett and the lawyers stayed focused, as they had to, while many of the press and public filed out for cigarettes and coffee. Craig stared blankly ahead, as he usually did.

CHAPTER 30

MY CAREER IN JOURNALISM has thrown up some seriously unpleasant incidents, but thankfully being asked to look at child porn had never been one of them. That changed at Craig Meehan's trial. To make sure that justice had been seen to be done, as it has to be, the court staff asked if a member of the press would look at the pictures that had been found on Craig's computer.

The court clerks first approached both myself and the Press Association's Dave Higgins. Both of us having young children, neither of us wanted to do it, but Dave bravely said he would, if no one else could be found. Seeing the look on his face, I had second thoughts about stepping back and nearly said I would do it, the macho instinct that thrives in newsrooms kicking in, wanting to test my belief that I am well-protected against shock, but then, common sense returned and I remembered that once material like that enters your mind it is there to stay and beyond your control, popping back to haunt you at times of its choosing, a demon unleashed into your subconscious.

Fortunately, a young woman reporter for a small news agency said she would do it. The courtroom was cleared for her to look at the images and her ashen face, when she emerged, told its own story. That incident was one of several which jolted the mind back onto just how serious a trial this was. Such a reminder was needed because the familiarity between the media and the Dewsbury Moor locals, the relaxed atmosphere between the two groups and the sometimes dry, dull nature of the evidence, meant the focus on the fact that this was a man accused of viewing appalling images of children being abused did, on occasion, become blurred.

Journalists get used to taking a step back from the horrors of a story and concentrating on their job, just as lawyers and court staff must become hardened to what they hear at work, able to treat it as their job and leave even the most harrowing passages of evidence behind in the courtroom when they go home at the end of the day, but there were other incidents which brought home the real reason we were all there. The court was told of some of the file names found on Craig's machine, such 'my virgin daughter', while as well as 'rape', 'incest' and 'daughter', the search words he had entered included 'teen hussy', and 'Lolita', a term that had been used 653 times.

Detective Constable James said that Lolita, the name of the young girl in the 1955 novel who becomes an object of infatuation for older man Humbert Humbert, is a frequently used term by someone searching for child porn. A transcript of Craig's interviews with the police, which began shortly after his arrest on April 2 and were held over several hours, was read to the court. He began by denying ever looking at any indecent images. He then introduced what would be the main plank of his defence, that he let several of his friends and neighbours use the computer whenever they needed to, hinting that anyone could have downloaded those images. When the 653 Lolita references were put to him by detectives, Craig said 'I don't go on any sites like that, I think it is disgusting.'

Various witnesses were also called to give their evidence, including two of Craig's cousins, Damien and Ryan Meehan. Both were close to Craig, and were regulars at 24 Moorside Road, although Damien said he had kept away from the place when it was swarming with press. The two looked strikingly similar, Damien a shorter, slimmer version of his brother, with his cropped black hair and prominent forehead, although unlike his brother his head was scar-free.

Both men said they spent long periods at number 24, Ryan sometimes there from 9am until 10pm. Wearing a red Manchester United home shirt, in contrast to his cousin's black away top, Ryan said he and Craig would download films and play X-box games, and he had never seen any child porn downloaded while at the house. He did, though, say the two had visited the website for the lad mag Nuts, and told the court the magazine's web address, www.nuts.co.uk.

Clearly not having heard of it, Mr Orbaum asked 'What is nuts.co.uk?'

'It is a men's magazine site,' Ryan said. 'Sport and funny stuff.' When asked if it had any pornographic content, Ryan replied: 'Topless girls.'

At the end of Ryan's evidence, in which he said nothing at all to implicate his cousin, it was revealed that when Craig was arrested for possessing the pictures, Karen had tried to pin them on Ryan. 'I knew this would happen. It is Ryan you need to be speaking to, he did it,' Karen told the arresting officers.

The police obviously did not share that view, because Ryan had never been arrested or been linked in any way at all with the pictures found on the computer. Karen's words appeared to be those of a woman desperate, at that point at least, to stand by her man and shift blame from him onto the next available target. The day he was arrested was the last time Craig would see Karen. He was kept in custody, and a couple of days later, Karen seemed to have decided Craig was to blame after all, ending her relationship with him.

The hearing was over for the day. The following morning Craig would be taking the stand to give the world, in his own words, his explanation of how those images came to be on his computer.

CHAPTER 31

THE NEXT MORNING I took the train to Dewsbury. As I sat there rattling through Batley and towards Dewsbury, past the strange spot where someone, for reasons unknown, has erected huge white letters spelling out HOLLYWOOD, I was thinking about the trial so far, the daily espresso I relied on to stave off "smelling salts moments" starting to kick in. Today Craig would enter the witness box. While his counsel, Mr Orbaum, had done his best to demonstrate that the evidence was all circumstantial, as circumstantial evidence went, it looked pretty powerful.

The fact that all the pictures bar one were downloaded on days when it could be proved Craig was not working, seemed pretty strong, and the court had also heard how a text message, using Craig's nickname Reggie, had been sent from the computer to a mobile phone the prosecution claimed belonged to his mother, Alice. Just moments after the text was sent, an image was downloaded.

The train doors juddered open at Dewsbury and I walked out onto the platform, the smell of bacon wafting tantalisingly from the tiny newsagent and sandwich shop tucked away inside the station. The courthouse was less than a minute away, across the road and down a sloping side-street, almost next door to the offices of the weekly paper The Dewsbury Reporter. BBC Look North's John Cundy was a few steps ahead, having left his car in the station car park.

In my hand was a portable video camera, ready for the moment when Craig left court, either as a convicted sex offender or with a not guilty verdict to his name. Local news reporters are no longer just print journalists, and our digital team wanted some footage of Craig leaving court or, ideally, an interview, as it was likely that even if Craig was found guilty, whatever sentence imposed would be less than the time he had already served on remand, meaning he would walk free at once.

The handycam had become something of a running joke with the court's security staff, whose numbers had been bolstered while the high-profile trial went on. Bags, coats and pockets were searched on the way in, and, as it is illegal to take recording equipment into court, I handed the camera over, getting a receipt in return. One of the guards in particular, a jovial, grey-haired, middle-aged man, began to chuckle even as he saw me coming. He had given me the nickname of 'the cameraman' on the first day, the large lenses on his spectacles seeming to bounce up and down as he shook with laughter.

I walked through the airport-style security arch, took the receipt and turned right past the security desk, noticeboards and broken public phone into the public waiting area. Dewsbury Magistrates Court is a relatively modern courtroom, the public areas quite light and airy, in contrast to some of the older, Victorian courts, which are often dark and gloomy.

The waiting area, a thinly-carpeted corridor about fifty feet long with seating and a few pot plants along the sides, was again packed with journalists and the familiar characters from the Moor. I walked into the tea bar at the end of the corridor, the WRVS volunteers in there friendly, chatty and smiley. As far as I saw, they treated everyone the same, not knowing whether they were defendant, lawyer, policeman or press.

I bought a coffee, poured from a fresh pot, took two sips and then saw everyone start to troop into court. I tried to ignore the scalding temperature and down it. My eyes must have started to water, as one of the women, spectacular gold hoops hanging from her ears, ordered me to hand the Styrofoam cup back to her. I obeyed, she tipped half the drink out and topped it up with cold water, then handed it back. A better solution than wasting it, so I gulped the extra caffeine down and headed into court.

Dewsbury Magistrates Court is modern throughout, the courtroom looking as if it could have been assembled from an Ikea flat-pack, with fittings of pine-effect wood, and shiny metal and glass. Even the fittings at the top of the dock, to stop anyone leaping out, were tasteful, made from thick, chrome-effect metal tubing rather than rough steel bars.

When Craig was brought in, he was still in that black Manchester United shirt and remembering his B.O., I had to wonder whether it or he had seen soap and water recently. The dock officers escorted him from the dock to the witness box in handcuffs, then unlocked them as he prepared to give his evidence.

Mr Orbaum questioned Craig first, asking him routine, scene setting questions about work and the day-to-day life he and Karen shared, before asking him about the state of their relationship, prompting a striking reply.

'It has been pretty good,' Craig said. 'But there have been times when we have argued because she has accused me of cheating on her. When I am at work I can be practically on my own all day, so when I come home I am quite tired and just want to go to bed. Karen has said I have somebody at work and I am cheating on her.'

Craig went on to say there was no basis to his partner's allegations, but at least half-a-dozen times they had driven him to walk out and stay at his mother's. Mr Orbaum then asked Craig to explain why, in police interviews, he had denied having any taste for porn, only for officers to find the stash of adult videos, leading to him to admit an interest, in the adult variety, when he was quizzed for the fifth time.

Craig replied that he had been confused by the detectives only using the word porn, claiming he feared they may have been referring to child porn. 'If they had said adult porn I would have agreed, but they never did,' he said.

'"Teen pussy", did you search for that?'

'No,' Craig said. He was unable to explain why the search terms were there, and claimed he was unable to even spell the word "Lolita". He had never used his machine to search for any sort of porn, instead mainly using it to look for music. He also claimed that

Police seal off and search the area surrounding Michael Donovan's flat. (March 14, 2008)

Photographers swarm to get their shot as Michael Donovan arrives for his first appearance at Dewsbury Magistrates Court. (March 18, 2008)

Shuttered up and behind bars: 24 Moorside Road after its occupants found themselves in custody.

Dewsbury Moor, a place where pedestrians have reclaimed their streets.

There are no bollards in Dewsbury Moor under the home-zone scheme –
only concrete penguins.

Richard Edwards first visited Dewsbury Moor expecting the missing child story to be wrapped up within 24 hours – instead, it ran through nearly a year of his life.

Westmoor Junior School. No children were in the mood to play while their schoolmate was away.

Richard Edwards and Julie Bushby outside the Moorside Tenants' and Residents' Association house, the unofficial Search for Shannon headquarters.

Bags of community spirit: resident volunteers were handed brown paper carriers full of Search for Shannon leaflets.

The left-hand
flat is the tiny
Lidgate Gardens
address where
Shannon was
kept prisoner for
24 long days.

A MESSAGE TO RESIDENTS ABOUT GIVING EVIDENCE

The trial at Leeds Crown Court can have an effect on all the residents of Dewsbury Moor. In February this year we all saw a massive effort by the residents and professionals of which we can all be very proud.

It is important that we don't let the facts that are coming out during the trial cause problems between residents.

In any court trial witnesses are called to tell the court what they know about the case. Some will have evidence that will be used by the defence, others will have evidence that will be used by the prosecution.

Residents need to understand that it's not about "taking sides", it's about telling facts as you know them.

No-one can choose which sort of evidence they have.

Don't let rumours or fear divide what we all know to be a strong, supportive community.

Dave Barnett
Inspector
Dewsbury/Mirfield NPT

This message to residents helped ensure the bonds forged during the search for Shannon stayed strong throughout and after the trial.

An old-
fashioned
community,
the Moor's
children still
play outdoors
– and will do
so from when
the sun comes
up......

156

.... to when it
goes down.

Dewsbury Moor was criticised for its supposed ugliness, but on a clear, sunny day, its view, for miles across the Pennines, is spectacular.

Shuttered and deserted. What will become of 24 Moorside Road?

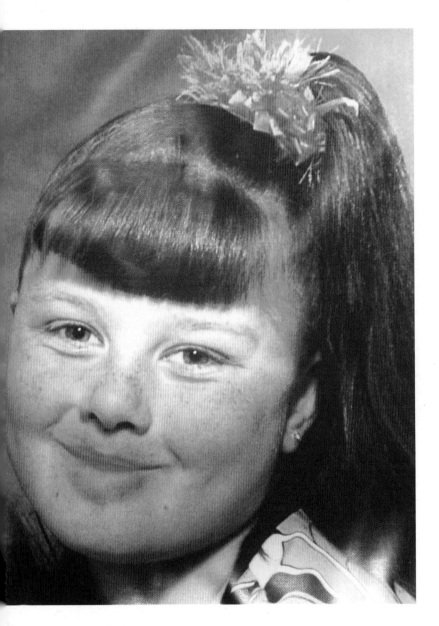

Shannon Matthews

some porn sites had popped up while searching for songs, sometimes when using the file-sharing facility Limewire, but that he deleted any porn, of any sort, straight away.

Other search words read out gave a small insight into life at number 24, as it turned out both Craig and Karen had put their own names through Google, while also looking for a particular type of crisps loved by Craig's mother.

He had also been searching for models of Eddie Stobart vehicles, the haulage trucks that have attracted a cult following. 'I collect toy cars,' Craig said.

During his examination by his own barrister, Craig had spoken clearly and calmly, but when he came under scrutiny from David Holderness, the prosecution counsel, his demeanour changed drastically. Whether it was intentional, a tactic he believed would rattle Mr Holderness, or whether it was just the pressure, Craig became combative, even aggressive in his approach, seeming to attempt verbal jousts with his questioner. At times he appeared to swallow deeply - was it the classic, giveaway gulp for air by someone who knows they are not telling the truth but is doing their best to hide it?

Mr Holderness, an amiable, quietly spoken man whose spectacles and thinning pate gave him the appearance of a comprehensive school science teacher, took Craig to task over his denial, then admission, that he had looked at porn sites. Then, as the questions and answers went backwards and forwards, he teased what, at the time, sounded like a major admission from Craig. He asked whether the legal, adult sites Craig had visited had ever brought him into contact with child porn. 'Not that I can remember,' Craig said.

'That is rather vague,' Mr Holderness said mildly.

'Well it is either say that or say something that I can't prove to be true and that would be a false statement.'.

'So it follows you might have accessed some child porn,' Mr Holderness said.

Craig's reply, which sounded as though it was halfway to being a confession, came: 'It does in a way, it doesn't in a way. If I come out with false statements that would be false.'

Late in the day, a deeply-tanned blonde woman, in her late 20s, and a mixed-race man, hair weaved into corn rows and a few years younger than his companion, made their way noisily into the public gallery. They sat a few seats away, but the strong smell of drink coming from them quickly hit my nostrils.

The cross-examination was still going on in front of them, and at a crucial point, I heard the man mutter something to one of the journalists, then, astonishingly, he pulled a mobile phone from his pocket and tried to take a picture of Craig, a blatant breach of the law.

The court clerk had spotted what was going on, and called security, who came and confiscated the man's phone, before throwing him out. If he had been in a Crown Court, the chances are he would have been sent to the cells. The journalist he spoke to later told colleagues the amateur cameraman had asked him how much the papers would pay for a picture of Craig in court. The reality is they would not pay anything, as the picture could not be used, but it is an example of how some people see the press as a cash cow, just waiting to be milked if the right opportunity comes along.

The afternoon half-gone, it was time to slip out of the court and phone my story through for the next day's paper. I sat in the tea bar, the shutters now down, the half-dozen tables empty, writing up my notes before ringing the office. As I was halfway through, out of the corner of my eye, I saw a man come in, stand next to the drinks machine and start fiddling around with a bag.

'What are you writing about then mate?' he asked, his voice a croak. I looked up. The man before me was probably only about thirty, but looked at least twenty years older, so ravaged was his face from hard drug use. His skin was a strange, sickly yellow-orange, pulled tightly back over his face like that of a shrunken corpse.

Presumably expecting a prison sentence after his court

appearance, he was sorting out old, dog-eared copies of Nuts and Zoo, the lads' magazines, and putting them into a drawstring bag. I told him about Craig's trial. He knew about the case, having read about it in the papers. 'He deserves to go where I'm going, the nonce,' he said, before plunging his hands down the front of his jeans.

The denim was surprisingly clean and crease-free, unlike his face, which resembled an old raisin, discovered months after it had fallen behind the fridge, any remaining moisture long since dried up. His hands still down his jeans, moving around as though he was chasing a ferret, his already lined face becoming even more screwed up, I went to return to my story, but had to ask the question. 'What are you doing there, mate?' I said.

His reply was matter-of-fact, as if he was telling me he was looking for his bus ticket, wallet or house keys. 'Just sticking a couple of diazepam under me foreskin. I'll be needing them tonight when I start doing my jail-time. I'll be rattling in there. Sticking them under your foreskin gives you the best chance.'

CHAPTER 32

THE MAN WAS WEARING A FLAT CAP and a grubby, blue-and-white anorak. With his left hand, he clutched a sandwich, on which he was munching while with his right hand, he relieved himself into the urinal. As I walked into the Gents, waiting to be called to hear the verdict on Craig's trial, the man looked around at me and briefly flinched, probably realising the way he was choosing to eat was pretty disgusting. Then, he must have shrugged inwardly, as he continued chomping away without any interruption to his flow.

I did what I needed to do, the sandwich man leaving as I did so, causing me no surprise when he walked straight out without washing his hands, then I washed my own and walked back into the waiting area which was full of debate over what the verdict would be. The general feeling among reporters was that there was enough evidence for him to be convicted, though not all, myself included, were convinced that he would be, as a level of doubt had definitely been cast on the prosecution evidence, the big question being just how strong that doubt was.

The trial had over-run the five days allocated, and the verdict and any sentencing had been held over into the following week. Extra police and police community support officers had been drafted in for the day, covering the front and back doors, ready should any trouble break out after the verdict, whichever way it went.

Bang on time, press and public were called back into court, the banter that there had been between the Moor residents and the media temporarily suspended, everyone understanding and respecting the seriousness of the moment. The locals occupied the front row of the public seating, most of those who had appeared, arm-in-arm outside the same court when Karen first appeared, were back again to see what was to become of her former partner.

DJ Bennett swept into court and told Craig to stand as he

delivered his judgement. It ran to ten printed pages.

He explained the background and reasons behind his decision, part of which saw him say he 'did not accept for one moment' that in the police interviews, Craig thought detectives were referring to child pornography whenever they mentioned porn. Damningly, he said he had judged that Craig had been lying, both when in the police interviews and then again, under oath, in the witness box, lies which, DJ Bennett said, 'tarnished his credibility considerably.' He went on to say that the piece of evidence which led him to believe that Craig did have a taste for child porn was that an image was downloaded the day after the computer was bought, at 7.28am. 'Who else would come round at that time in the morning?' DJ Bennett asked.

The defence's attempt to cast doubt on whether Craig had downloaded the images, because of the large number of people who could have used the computer, was discounted, as the judge found that very few people, if anyone, would have been able to get onto the machine at a time the house was empty, and also that visitors to the home often used Karen's computer, instead of Craig's.

'The Crown has painted a convincing and overwhelming picture that it was this defendant downloading indecent images,' DJ Bennett said. As the judgement was being read out, Craig listened, his face expressionless apart from the odd blink behind his spectacles, confirmation of his guilt coming after several minutes, when the judge convicted him on eleven charges. Craig remained impassive as he officially became a sex offender, the fact he was cleared of the twelfth charge, the picture on his mobile phone, making no difference to his fate. At sentencing, this was acknowledged by DJ Bennett, who said: 'The conviction for these offences will be further publicised. Such cases often attract publicity, but your case - as is demonstrated by the enormous media attention - will be far more than most. Undoubtedly as a result of the events of this year your life has changed forever. Life cannot go back to what it was before February 19. Over the coming months you are going to face some difficult circumstances.'

The judge reminded Craig of the horrific effect the making of those images would have had on those children, saying: 'The damage that has been caused to the children in these photographs is unimaginable. That is why Parliament regards these matters as so serious and why there is widespread social abhorrence of such offences. The most vulnerable in our society have to be protected.'

He then pronounced sentence: twenty weeks in jail - less time than he had already spent behind bars, so he would be freed at once - and a comprehensive seven-year sexual offences prevention order which, among other things, banned Craig from possessing photographs of children under sixteen unless it is with permission of the child's parents.

As the sentence was read out, there were loud sobs from the public gallery as Amanda Hyett burst into floods of tears, while neighbour Petra Jamieson tried to comfort her. The case was officially closed, and, after DJ Bennett had left the court, the press followed as quickly as they could to send their stories through. I rang Gillian Haworth to confirm the conviction, so a very brief story could be placed on the YEP's website, to be updated later, then dashed to pick up the video camera, ready to catch some footage of Craig when he was walked back into society, technically a free man again after 166 days behind bars, but it was a very limited and vulnerable form of freedom; the press and angry members of the public were now his jailers rather than a man in a white shirt with a long key-chain hanging from his belt.

Outside, the press pack seemed unsure where to stand and wait, trying to guess whether Craig would walk out of the front door or be escorted from the rear entrance, usually only used for bringing in remand defendants or for taking those convicted away to begin their sentences. Amanda, her face and eyes still red with tears, was interviewed as she left, and insisted Craig would always be part of her family. 'He's my only brother, he's my blood, I didn't choose him to do that,' she said.

A friendly policeman, who was probably keen to keep the crowd of press and public in one place where they could be more easily managed, confirmed that Craig would be leaving by the back way, and around thirty journalists assembled there, together with half-a-dozen people from the Moor and a handful more who had no direct connection to the case, there to satisfy their own curiosity at the end of a high-profile trial.

As we waited, I spoke to some of Craig's former neighbours. Natalie Brown, wife of "Scouse" Pete, said she felt 'confused and disturbed' by the verdict. She and her husband had been close to Craig and Karen, and Pete at one point had described Craig as his best mate, trusting him so much that he let Craig baby-sit their children.

'I don't want to,' Natalie said, 'but I can't help but wonder if he has been looking at them. My daughter is only nine, and like girls her age she loves to dance. She has seen the way the girls dance on the telly and she dances quite seductively, she says she wants to be a pole dancer. He has been there when she has danced, it really worries me to think he has been watching her doing that.'

Julie Bushby said the Dewsbury Moor community was disgusted and disappointed with Meehan's crimes, and warned he would be unable to ever return there. 'If he comes back up to the Moor, I don't think he'll get very far,' she said. 'He won't be able to go back.'

As with the fruitless stake-out of Dewsbury Police Station, when it was thought Karen was being questioned there, every bit of activity near the back door caused a flurry of activity amongst the journalists, with the communal at-ease position being adopted again when the pack saw that the car leaving was simply a member of the court's staff heading out on their lunch hour.

Then, suddenly, it became obvious that Craig was on his way. The doors opened and stayed open, and an unmarked police car, escorted by a marked car, lights flashing and siren on, sped from under the shutters. In the back of the anonymous vehicle was Craig, for some reason covering his head with a jacket, his mother Alice sitting next to him. Like a football crowd when a goal has been scored, the press surged forward, just a few seconds to get the image they had waited well over an hour for, and then he was gone. The next task was to find out where.

CHAPTER 33

PAEDOPHILES HAVE TO LIVE SOMEWHERE, but, understandably, no one wants them for a next-door-neighbour. The reality is that many people will already have a sex offender of some sort living not too far away – the Shannon inquiry revealed that there are hundreds in the Kirklees area alone – but, generally, the current situation, in which the authorities know where the offenders are but the public does not, seems to work pretty well. Those with relatively long memories will remember the fallout from a Sunday newspaper's name and shame campaign, several years ago, in which innocent people had their homes attacked, a mob came very close to rioting in Portsmouth and a couple of knuckle-draggers even managed to attack and vandalise the home of a paediatrician.

This was all in my mind as I set out to try to trace Craig. Despite his crimes, the last thing I wanted was to cause a mob to appear outside wherever he was staying, baying for his blood. I settled for looking for him, in the hope of printing an exclusive interview but leaving his address out of it. The ethics of publishing the thoughts of a paedophile, if I found him, were also playing on my mind – no other such offenders have been given space in the YEP, as far as I can remember – but I had instructions to follow and have to admit to getting caught up in the moment, the thrill of the chase, wanting to see the story through as far as it could possibly go.

Sources had given me an address on Dewsbury Moor that it had been thought Craig might be taken to, but they later told me that place had been ruled out as the family members living there had children aged under eighteen, making it off limits for a child sex offender. It also seemed highly unlikely to me that the authorities would allow him to return to the Moor, partly because of the risk to his own safety but also because of the danger of sparking a big outbreak of disorder.

With nothing to go on, where to start? The only place was back at the Moor, to knock on doors and ring contacts, in the hope someone knew, or had heard something. As it had done through all its previous traumas, the Moor was getting on with life, the locals having the daily grind to deal with, but all were well aware of what had been going on a couple of miles down the road in their local courthouse, and all were clear they did not want to see Craig Meehan's face ever again.

I parked on Moorside Road, a short distance from Julie Bushby's home and a set of the home-zone concrete penguins. The schools had closed for the day, and parents were starting to bring their children home, others, already back, wheeling around on bicycles or kicking a football around, a misplaced shot making me jump as it thudded off the windscreen of my car, shaking me from my thoughts about how to trace a man who could be anywhere in the huge county of Yorkshire or even further afield. I asked three people in their twenties, a man and two women, a gaggle of small schoolchildren swarming around them as they headed home, what their thoughts were about Craig's case.

'Back again are you?' the man half-sneered, not breaking his stride.

'If he comes back here, he'll get his head kicked in,' one of his female companions said, also without stopping and declining to give her name. I then recognised her, as she was a relative of Shannon's best friend, Megan, and had agreed to be interviewed by me when Shannon was missing. She was much friendlier then, so press fatigue had either kicked in or perhaps she had not liked the first story.

A woman in a nearby garden was much more willing to talk though, introducing herself as Elaine Speight, gold on her ears and around her neck, leaning on her garden gate as I approached, her muscular Staffordshire Bull terrier prowling in and out of her legs, happy to make clear her views on the form of justice that should come Craig's way. Elaine, her teenage daughter standing a few feet behind her, said: 'He wants leathering. My dog does not normally bite but he would do if he ever came back here. We've all got kids, why would we want a paedophile here?'

As she spoke, my phone beeped with a text message from a Shannon story contact, whose information had been impeccable all the way through. The text told me that Craig had been taken to Keighley, a former mill town in a remote part of West Yorkshire, nestled in a valley beneath the moors of Bronte Country. The source had heard he was being sheltered by Karen's cousin, Susan Howgate, and her husband, Graham, a couple who had supported Craig and Karen while their little girl was away, helping with the search for her. It seemed strange that his ex-partner's relatives would take him in, but I did remember a comment from Graham about Craig.

'Everyone knows Reggie. Everyone has got plenty of time for Reggie,' he had said, but that, of course, was long before his tastes in pornography were revealed. The source gave me a phone number for a relative of the Howgates, who, when I rang, said they had also heard Craig was there, was furious about it, and agreed to give me Graham and Susan's address.

'They've got kids in there, there is no way he should be allowed to live with them,' the relative said. Keighley is not too far away from Dewsbury, in terms of distance, but in reality Keighley is not that close to anywhere, out on a limb and accessible mostly by winding, single carriage A and B roads, the rush hour traffic bound to add a bit of extra time. Still, it was a route I had never driven before, and I was quite looking forward to seeing the beautiful bleakness of West Yorkshire's moors. I rang my newsdesk and picture desk to let them know what I was up to, and first swung the car west towards Huddersfield, the traffic heavy at first, but quickly thinning out as I took the road north-west, Brighouse way, gaining height as I went, stone walls and farmers' fields at the side of the road, cows standing ankle-deep in the glorious green grass, thoughtfully chewing away as ever, unbothered by the steady drizzle.

The route took a right for Queensbury, through the superbly

named place of Stone Chair, and continuing to climb and the traffic slower now, tractors on the road and quite a lot of roadworks, the dreaded temporary traffic lights popping up all too regularly, causing jams as they closed the already clogged two lanes down to just one. It was one of those drives where the place you are heading to seemed to be getting no closer, until, finally, there were the outskirts of Keighley, the relics of industry still obvious, a couple of tower blocks close to the town centre, but much of what I could see from the car window looking quite attractive, certainly in a stunning setting. A town that might have a fair bit of money here and there but also some bad deprivation, poverty often seeming to go off the radar when it exists in rural areas or middle-of-nowhere spots.

The address I had been given was not far from the town centre, taking me into a grid-iron pattern of terraced houses, stone built and seeming to be in a good condition, the jewellery shops in many of the streets, side-by-side with someone's home a telltale sign this was a mainly Asian community. I was looking for the street name as I drove slowly, then spotting The Mirror's Lucy Thornton passing me in the opposite direction, us clocking each other, smiling and flashing the headlights, pulling over for a chat.

It turned out that Lucy had been given the same address as me, though we didn't ask each other if it had come from the same contact, so we agreed to knock on the door together to save the Howgates from being bothered twice. Their house was on a pedestrianised part of the street, the front room window above eye level, the front door a couple of steep steps up, a vase on a shelf and a couple of pieces of art all that was visible of the front room, impossible to see if there were any seats, or if anyone was sitting at them. There was no answer to the knock at first, but we knocked again, the television on loud, and we heard the muffled noises of someone approaching a front door, it swung open and there was Susan, a look of puzzled half-recognition towards me, as we had spoken several times when Shannon was away but she would have no reason to remember my face.

She looked younger than I had remembered, perhaps because when I had seen her on the Moor her face had always been pinched and blue with cold, her hair quite short, her jaw and teeth prominent and proud, a fresh, unsmoked roll-up cigarette between her fingers. There was no point beating around the bush, so straight away I introduced myself, said why we were there, that we had heard Craig was staying with them and was it true? Susan looked puzzled, shook her head, replied that she didn't know what we were talking about, Craig wasn't coming, there were no plans for him to, never had been. Her teenage son appeared, the reason the relative who had given me the address had been so angry at the thought of Craig going there. The son had always been a confident, friendly lad when I met him during the Shannon search and he was so again, interested to have a couple of reporters turning up on his doorstep but as baffled as his mother about our Craig idea.

Like her son, Susan had also always been friendly towards the press, and, despite having her evening interrupted, she was happy to talk again, probably curious where our information had come from although thankfully she didn't ask, until Graham appeared over his wife's shoulder. He had been welcoming in the past but that was long gone now. His face full of fury, he was pointing and swearing, telling us where to go, that he had moved to Keighley to get away from the press and now there we were on his doorstep,

Lucy and I were ready to say goodbye and leave but Susan told us to ignore her husband, trying to push him back inside, still keen to chat to us. Eventually Graham did go back inside, only to pop up again in the front window, still raging, waving his arms about and shouting, the point when he banged on the window letting us know it really was time to leave, even though Susan still said we should stay. We thanked her, apologised for the bother and retreated to our cars, ringing our bosses to report the dead-end, starting the drive back home after a long and busy day.

In a way, I was relieved not to have to tackle the ethical question of speaking to a child sex offender, but I was disappointed not to get the story, having come so far and believing I was so close. Craig's trail went cold after that, although one of the Sunday tabloids had him very much in its sights, printing a couple of strange stories, clearly knowing where his safe house was, probably after using a private detective. I did keep in touch with his mother, Alice, but the conversations we had were fairly neutral, until, just over a week after he was convicted, she told me that her son had come close to making a second suicide attempt, his first being in the late stages of the search for Shannon.

Alice said her son was still in love with Karen, and the pressure of the loss of his father, the Shannon saga and his exposure as a pervert had driven him to the edge. She told me: 'I had to keep talking to him, I was telling him what I went through and how I pulled myself out of it. Eventually, he came around.' Alice said she thought her son would like to see Karen, but that he had not tried to visit her in New Hall Prison. He would see her again – but only through the newspaper and television artists impressions as she went on trial, accused of kidnapping her own daughter.

CHAPTER 34

THE SIZE AND PROFILE OF A TRIAL at Leeds Crown Court can be judged from the number of broadcasting vans squeezed onto the supposedly pedestrianised pavement in front of the courthouse, in Oxford Row. For the start of Karen and Mick's trial, there were so many vans they had started to spill out onto Westgate, lining up nose to tail almost as far as the Magistrates' Court, about a minute's walk away. Where the vans ended, the photographers began, grouped together in a phalanx as always, this time, for some reason, having chosen to stand in a long line, rather than bunching up, spreading halfway across the red tiles of the walkway, up to twenty pairs of eyes watching every movement, scanning the street in case anyone of interest should appear and try to slip into court unnoticed.

It was Armistice Day, the scheduled start of Karen and Mick's trial, and inevitably it had been delayed, put back nearly four hours to 2pm. Neil Hyett arrived at court a split-second after me, the photographers clocking him in an instant, calling his name for the shot, Neil turning briefly to oblige before ducking in through the revolving glass doors. We shook hands, me not quite understanding Neil's claim that the trial had begun the day before, him telling me that neither he nor Amanda were to be called as witnesses, then we were at the security arch, emptying our pockets of all metal, waiting to be called through, my bag searched, the hand-held scanner wafted up and down my body, before I was nodded inside, ready to go to work.

Leeds Crown Court has a press room, tucked away in a corner of the building, a handy retreat and hideaway for journalists, the YEP having its own phone line fitted there, a hotline straight to the newsdesk. Around the rest of the room there were a couple of tables and chairs, an ancient kettle and filing cabinet, some ageing papers and magazines, the back wall dominated by a huge noticeboard where any orders made by judges restricting the reporting of a case are pinned. In not-too-distant days the room would have been filled with cigarette smoke, gone now of course. Olwen Dudgeon, the Yorkshire Post's excellent court reporter, the odd agency staffer were the regular faces, but the numbers greatly increased on big trial days.

This being one of the biggest of big trial days, journalists from every national paper except The Independent and The Daily Sport were there, as well as plenty from the regional press and the news agencies. There was plenty of chatter going back and forwards, nowhere to sit. Olwen Dudgeon reminded me of an order in place that could restrict any description of Karen's appearance in the dock, thankfully revoked by the judge, Mr Justice McCombe, minutes after we arrived in court. There was a definite feeling of anticipation in the air, and as ten-to-two arrived, everyone trooped to court 12, an overspill room set up next door with a videolink so all the journalists there could find a seat.

The chatter outside was hushed, people respecting where they were; journalists, police officers and Moor locals exchanging greetings, though not everyone from the Moor was there as some were to be called as witnesses later. Everyone walked into court and took their seats, as the lawyers glided about, their black robes and wigs looking right in court even though they would look ridiculous elsewhere.

Then there was the clank of a door and jangle of a key chain and Karen and Mick were brought into the dock, at the back of the room, right in the judge's eyeline and behind a high sheet of Perspex, the two defendants staring straight ahead, not looking at each other, with a young, female dock officer sitting between them. Karen looked relaxed, smiling at her guard, chatting as she was handed a cup of water, Mick was not saying a word, his glazed eyes not seeming to see anything. There was a single, sombre knock and everyone stood as the judge walked into court. The trial was underway... or not.

The lawyers had a few pieces of housekeeping to work through, one of them asking the judge to lift the reporting restrictions, and of course there was the big task of selecting and swearing in the jury. The main prosecuting barrister, Julian Goose QC, asked the judge to retire briefly to check some paperwork, his Lordship agreed and everyone again sprang to their feet as he rose, returning his bow to the court, and not moving a muscle until he had exited left and the door had swung shut behind him.

Half-an-hour later the door rapped again and the judge returned, scarlet and black trim robes swishing as he walked to his seat, a quick bow this time, taking the weight off and asking for the jurors to be brought in, the twelve men and women chosen from a large pool of potential jurors called to meet their public duty of jury service, some probably feeling daunted as they realised which trial they might be involved in, others excited at the thought, hoping they would be picked. The judge first asked if any of the potential jurors had a good reason for not being able to sit on the case, due to last about a month, and surprising number of hands went up, at least ten.

The judge called them, one-by-one, to stand in front of him and explain why they could not serve. The scene was strangely like children queuing up at Father Christmas's grotto, those in the line slightly nervous, a man wearing red, white fur on his cuffs waiting for them at the end, the white hair on his head, his wig, rather than on his chin. It must have been intimidating, having to speak up in front of a packed courtroom, and trying to convince a judge why you should be excused from joining a jury in his court. The first woman to approach was clearly nervous, speaking quietly, her excuse of a pre-booked holiday in December, not deemed good enough, the judge and lawyers saying the trial would definitely be over by then. The second woman, a short, timid creature, sidling up, her already low confidence knocked by what she had just seen, peered up at the judge, hands gripping the top of his desk, getting more change out of him and being put on standby to be excused.

The judge remained polite and friendly with all of them, while making them realise how important a duty jury service is. He even cracked a joke about one man's ski-jacket, and let him off when he discovered that the man was on a jury a few months ago, but he was less sympathetic to a financial services type who insisted his company could not manage without him. The judge told the young high-flyer that they would just have to manage. Eventually, the seven men and five women - twelve good Yorkshiremen and women, and true, were chosen, and were ready to hear the case, the judge warning them to avoid reading any outside publicity about it, not to talk about it with family or friends, and then sending them home for the night, asking them to arrive promptly the next day, the fate of two people resting in their hands.

CHAPTER 35

ANYONE THINKING that the trial of Karen Matthews and Mick Donovan could not live up to the astonishing trail of events that had led them to share the dock in court, was way off the mark. When the case did get underway, it was with what must have been one of the most jaw-dropping opening days ever heard at Leeds Crown Court. In the British genteel, ultra-courteous legal tradition, Mr Justice McCombe, speaking in deep, rich tones, could have been opening an everyday civil dispute between two neighbours over access to a driveway when he addressed the jury and said: 'Mr Goose is going to tell you some more about this case.'

Prosecuting Counsel Julian Goose, then began outlining the prosecution's evidence, detailing several Shannon stories that were already public knowledge, but many more that weren't, and by the time he finished speaking, even the most hardened of hacks was left appalled at the casual brutality meted out to a little girl.

Mr Goose painted a picture of a conspiracy between Karen and Mick, both of them equally involved, to hide Shannon and then have her "turn up" when the newspaper reward money on offer reached £50,000, a bounty they would then share between them. Statements from Mick's police interviews, which were read to the court, claimed that Karen had spotted Mick one day as he was driving onto the Dewsbury Moor estate to visit his sister, Alice, Craig Meehan's mum. Alice had recently lost her husband, and, despite having been estranged from Mick for several years, the two had grown closer through his offers to help and support Alice through her grief.

As he tried to follow the court proceedings, Mick, who has learning difficulties, was aided by a person who sat in the dock with him. Together they followed what was being said with the aid of what appeared to be a word-for-word transcript. Mick's claim was that Karen, pushing her younger daughter in her pram, had flagged him down as he drove to visit Alice, then staying at her daughter Caroline's house, in Moorside Avenue. After looking around to see if anyone was watching, she had leaned in through the open car window and said that she needed 'a big favour' but was unable to talk then instead asking for a meeting at another time, without Craig there. The two then met at a busy café in town, with the little girl again along for the ride, a witness too young to understand or explain what was being plotted before her. Karen, it was alleged, asked Mick if he would take care of her son for her. Mick said he didn't know him, but that he did know he was a regular runaway, the police bringing him home each time he vanished, so Karen then asked him if he would instead take care of Shannon; 'there would be money in it for him.'

According to Mick, the idea was that Shannon would stay at his flat, Karen would report her missing and the two would then watch and wait until the reward money reached the £50,000 mark. Mick claimed to police that he had said he wasn't interested, but Karen threatened him, saying she would set three lads onto him if he didn't do as she wanted. He did not reveal their names, but told the detectives he recognised the names Karen reeled off to him. One of them had previously stabbed a man to death, and Mick was scared of what would happen to him if he refused to do as Karen said.

With that threat hanging over him, Mick claimed that he said he would do it but rejected Karen's offer of a share of the spoils, to which she said that if he didn't do it, he 'would be dead'. This alleged threat formed the main plank of Mick's defence, justifying his claim that he acted under duress, in fear of what would happen to him if he refused. That defence was rejected by the prosecution, who claimed he was a willing partner, having had ample opportunities to ask the police for help during the twenty-four days that Shannon was at his flat, but took none of them.

Mick claimed that Karen next produced a large piece of paper on which was written a date and a time when he was supposed to wait for Shannon. The date was 19 February 2008, and Shannon was to be lured into Mick's car by the promise of a trip to a funfair, an offer that would appeal to any child, but for a girl of Shannon's deprived background, it must have felt like her birthday had come early. The plan worked, Shannon got into Mick's car, and he then told this young, trusting girl, that the fair had been cancelled because of the fog, and that instead she was going to visit Mick's house. It was the beginning of a twenty-four day incarceration for her.

As time went on, Mick claimed, and as he read the papers and watched the news, he wanted to take Shannon back but was scared of the threats from Karen hanging over him. She kept in contact by telephone, updating Mick on how much reward money was available. When it hit that £50,000 jackpot, Mick was to drop Shannon at one end of Dewsbury market and then make his way to the other end, where he would "find" her, take her to the police station and later claim the reward. It did not seem to have dawned on either of the pair that police suspicions would instantly have been aroused by Shannon turning up in this way. In a final touch, like an extract from a very low-rent spy movie, Mick claimed that Karen told him to dispose of his written instructions from her by flushing them down the toilet.

CHAPTER 36

WHATEVER THE TRUTH of Mick's claims, one thing was undeniable: Shannon had ended up at Mick's flat, and it was there, the prosecution alleged, that things took a very sinister turn. It had been revealed at an earlier court hearing – although the media were then banned from reporting it – that Shannon had been drugged while being held in captivity, although the type and amount of the medication she had been given was not detailed.

At the trial, the world learned that Shannon had been given two drugs: Temazepam - the powerful sleeping tablet given to insomniacs and popular among drug users for the ultra-drowsy, almost trance like state it can trigger; and the travel sickness tablet Traveleeze, which contains active ingredients that can also cause tiredness. Temazepam is so strong that Shaun Ryder, the former frontman of The Happy Mondays, once notorious for his drug use, immortalised Temazepam during the height of its black market popularity in the mid 1990s, when he wrote the song *Tramazi Party* for his then-band, Black Grape. If the drug affected the burly Ryder so much that it moved him to write a song about it, it must have floored a skinny primary schoolgirl who stood less than five feet tall.

Even worse was the revelation that tests of Shannon's hair showed that she had been given Temazepam long before she found herself in Mick's flat, possibly over a nine-month period. It was proof that someone, probably Karen, had been giving Shannon the drug while she was home at Moorside Road, in all likelihood to remove any chance of Shannon waking up and disturbing her mother during the evening or night.

More frightening even than that, was the police evidence that when they raided Mick's flat, they found a long strap with a noose-like band at the end, which the prosecution claimed was used to restrain Shannon like a dog whenever Mick made his regular trips to the shops or collect his prescriptions. As a diagram produced in court showed, the tether, knotted round a roof beam in the loft, had been measured to allow access to certain parts of the flat such as the toilet, while keeping the front door agonisingly out of reach. No one in that courtroom who heard of that terrible device for the first time could have avoided feelings of horror, revulsion and immense pity for Shannon.

The final revelation from inside Mick's flat seemed almost tame in comparison, that he – and probably Karen – had drawn up a list of "do's and don'ts" for Shannon to follow while she was held there. The rules, found written on a piece of paper on the top of the television, were:

You must not make any noise and bang your feet;

You must not go near the windows;

You must not do or get anything without me being there;

Keep the TV volume low - up to volume eight;

You can play Super-Mario and watch some DVDs.

The final rule read simply 'IPU', which, Mr Goose said, was a code agreed between Shannon and Karen for 'I Promise You.'

Those three short words were a heartbreaking reminder of the immense trust that a child places in a parent, and will continue to do so even if that trust takes a battering. That trust, the prosecution alleged, had been abused and exploited by Karen Matthews as she carried out her plan, knowing the three-letter code would act as a reminder to Shannon that everything would turn out all right, because mummy had said it would.

As she listened to the allegations against her, Karen kept up the stance she had taken from her early crown court appearances, sullen, sulky and disdainful. Staring straight ahead towards the judge, she seemed to hold the court in contempt, as if it had no right to be making such claims against her. That contrasted sharply with her demeanour when the court was not in session, when she looked relaxed and smiling as she sipped from a cup of water occasionally chatting with the dock officers.

Karen's attitude changed drastically – if temporarily – at the simple press of a button on a DVD player. This twenty-first century trial, held following an ultra-scientific police inquiry, was using technology that would never have been seen in a court even fifteen years ago. Now the jurors had their own television monitors, and a large flatscreen television showed visual evidence to the press and public, including computer-generated images of the inside of Mick's flat and the tether and noose. To illustrate the prosecution's claims about the differences in Karen's behaviour in private and when performing for the television cameras, a montage of many of her TV interviews was shown to the court, including several in which she tearfully appealed for Shannon to come home, or for whoever was holding the girl to let her go. On and on they went, the whole sequence lasting more than fifteen minutes, while Karen, her face half-hidden behind her curtain of long red hair, stared down into a corner of the dock, avoiding even a glimpse of the footage that offered a stark reminder of all that had gone before and how spectacularly it had unravelled.

CHAPTER 37

THE OPENING EXCHANGES HAD BEEN DRAMATIC ENOUGH. But halfway through the first day came a development that looked like it might see the whole case collapse, sending Karen and Mick back to their remand cells until, months down the line, a retrial date could be arranged.

I went back into court after, in the fabulously old-fashioned language used in court, the luncheon adjournment, to be told by the Yorkshire Post's Olwen Dudgeon that all members of the press had been asked to gather in the overflow annexe for an announcement. Intrigued and slightly confused, we joined the grim-faced press men and women, to listen to a member of the Crown Prosecution Service's staff whose expression and tone of voice were equally serious. The gist of the lecture was difficult to understand at first but, as she paused, a conversation between Mr Goose and the judge was relayed into the room through the videolinks, in which the prosecuting counsel said: 'Any interview of any witnesses before the trial may potentially derail the trial. They (the defence) have said they cannot be expected to cross-examine witnesses unless they know everything that witness has had to say.'

At the words 'derail the trial', the room fell deadly silent, and for a couple of seconds, it looked as though the judge was about to throw the case out. Under British law, regardless of what they had been accused of, at that point the defendants were still presumed to be innocent and entitled to a fair trial. Then, just as the trial looked to be teetering on the brink, the next witness statement was produced and things carried on as normal. Confusion reigned, as we fired questions at the CPS staffers, who looked just as baffled as everyone else.

It eventually turned out that the defence had lodged a query about reporters interviewing - and possibly paying - witnesses before the trial had begun to gather material that would be used in the aftermath of the verdicts. The defence barristers said they were concerned that a witness who had agreed to an interview might have said something different to the reporter than they subsequently said in the witness box, potentially prejudicing the defence. It was a possible barrier to a fair hearing, a loophole that could have led to an appeal and future retrial, but the judge then made an unprecedented request, leaving some veteran journalists red-faced with anger.

The request, relayed by Mr Goose, asked every print and broadcast journalist to supply a list of everyone on the witness register who they had interviewed. If it was thought that those interviews might impact on the witnesses' evidence to the court, the lawyers would then wish to see the reporter's notebook or the 'raw' television footage.

However, such a request struck at the heart of the long-established principles of the freedom of the press and a reporter's right to protect the confidentiality of his sources. A reporter's notebook is sacrosanct, and reporters have gone to jail in the past rather than reveal their sources. If any press interview, despite promises of confidentiality, could be revealed in open court, many people would be far less willing to speak to the press and our ability to cover the news - particularly the stories that powerful interests might prefer to keep hidden - would be seriously compromised. It was a matter of principle, but there was also anger that such a request had not been made weeks, if not months earlier, during the time both defence and prosecution had to prepare their cases.

I breathed a sigh of relief that I had dropped an idea of writing to Karen with the aim of interviewing her in prison; had it happened, it could have been a major issue. Instead, I knew there was only one interview with a witness in my notebook, merely talking about the way the community had coped during the Shannon saga. I decided to get on with covering the trial, leaving any decisions about how to respond to the request until I had spoken to my editor, Paul Napier. However some media colleagues, mainly from the national media, declared there and then that they would be fighting the judge's request, and dashed off to ring their editors and ask for barristers to be despatched.

While this flurry of activity continued in the background, the trial resumed - like a football match continuing while there is a disturbance in the crowd. A statement from Mick's older sister, Maria Harper, was read in court, in which she said that her brother had been educated at what was then known as a "special school", and that he had been a storyteller and a fantasist since his teenage years, when he was also a repeat runaway. 'I don't know why he wanted to be someone else,' Mrs Harper said. The two had been estranged from each other for a time, but had made contact again a few years ago, though her brother's taste for tall tales had not gone away. 'He would still fantasise and tell stories about anything and everything, like saying he could fix televisions and radios like my dad.'

As Mrs Harper's statement was read out, an old lady, perfectly turned out in buttoned-up green jacket, tightly permed grey hair and carrying a shopping bag, wandered in, seemingly unaware of where she was, and mistakenly made a beeline for the lawyer's benches, before an alert court official leapt to her feet and steered her towards the public gallery. Her visit was one of a few lighter moments, another coming with the playing of a strange montage of CCTV footage of Mick on his errands around Dewsbury and Batley, the awkward, jerky pictures of him going into shop after shop, carrying no sound and played out to a totally silent courtroom, like a 1920s silent movie that had been washed with colour, triggered stifled laughs and a whispered joke from just behind the press benches that 'he likes his shopping trips doesn't he?'

Far more seriously, details emerged about Karen's behaviour after Mick had been arrested, revealing that she was placed straight in police sights by her alleged accomplice, who, Mr Goose said, told the police 'Get Karen down here, we're sharing the money, £50,000,' as he sat handcuffed in the back of the police van. It turned out that the period in which Karen came under intense local suspicion, between March 16 and April 6, coincided with heightened police suspicions, as she was interviewed under caution – though not arrested – four days after Shannon was found. Even before that interview started, Karen was said to have told detectives, 'I know this is because of what he has said about me, we are getting blamed for this and we have done nothing. I'll tell you what, when me and Craig had a tiff I went down to his mum's, he were there and wanted me to go to his flat with my kids, that's why he's chosen Shannon.'

From there, Karen's story changed like the wind, with her first claiming she had never met Mick in that café, nor had anything to do with the kidnap plan or him keeping Shannon at his flat. She said that she loved Craig and had never considered leaving him. After her arrest, the picture changed with Karen admitting she had spoken to Mick the night before Shannon vanished to ask his advice about Craig, who, she claimed, had been violent towards her. Mick's advice, Karen claimed, was to throw Craig out, and she had arranged for Mick to collect Shannon and would then meet him later with the three other young children in tow. She doesn't seem to have thought about where she would go after that. She then said she had second thoughts about leaving Craig and had reported Shannon missing to explain away the fact she hadn't come home that day.

Later interviews saw Karen blaming anyone and everyone, apart from herself. On April 7 she claimed that Amanda Hyett was behind it all, then two days later she changed her mind and said Craig was the ringleader, telling a security guard that 'If I'm going down he's coming down with me.' A few days after that, she told police that Mick, Craig and Amanda were in it together. Karen claimed that she had nothing to do with it, but had been living in fear of Craig who had forced her to say everything she had previously told the police.

Other than Karen's allegations, there was no evidence whatsoever that Craig or Amanda had anything to do with the plot, and Mr Goose claimed that Karen's attempts to implicate them merely demonstrated that she was a 'proven, consummate liar . . . she has managed to conjure up tears in an effort to convince her audience she was telling the truth, when, in fact, it was a barefaced lie.'

If all that sounded bad enough for Karen, the day came to a close with some highly damaging evidence from Natalie Brown, who said Karen would behave one way for the cameras, and another when she was in private. It was a description that fitted my own experience with Karen, though understandably, it appeared that Karen was even more prepared to let things slip when behind closed doors with trusted friends than a reporter she barely knew.

Mr Goose said that Natalie thought Karen was acting, dissolving in tears when in public, while behaving quite normally in private, laughing, joking and even play-fighting with Craig.

CHAPTER 38

THE T-SHIRTED MAN STOOD OUTSIDE THE CROWN COURT, unbothered by the constant drizzle, a highly libellous allegation against a member of the legal profession spelled out in huge black letters on the white background, like the "Frankie Says…" shirts that were everywhere when pop band Frankie Goes to Hollywood briefly ruled pop music's roost in the mid-1980s. With jet black hair and an aggrieved expression on his lobster pink, pockmarked face, the man was handing out tiny strips of paper carrying a website address, claiming he had been on the receiving end of a miscarriage of justice at the hands of this particular lawyer. Later spotted inside the court, a leather jacket firmly buttoned up to hide the claim on his top half, he was just one of the many unusual characters attracted to the crown court.

The campaigner knew he had a captive audience. Security protecting the entrance to Leeds Crown Court is tight, with two walk-through metal detectors, a guard standing in front and behind, the first to search bags and make sure pockets have been emptied of metal objects, the second to run a hand-held metal detector over the court visitor from head to toe. The building, which looks small from the outside but inside is a warren of corridors and doors, with more than a dozen crown courtrooms spread across two upper floors and several more on the ground floor, where the mysterious, often private business of the Combined Court Centre is carried out.

That number of court rooms entails a huge number of people and, at peak morning times, the queue to get through security can snake a long way down Oxford Row. It offers useful cover to anyone hoping to approach unseen by the photographers, but only until the moment when they realise that they also have to wait their turn, and they become easy targets, either posing for the lenses or standing there awkwardly, pretending not to notice the barrage of photographers' flashes.

This morning, the queue was moving slowly, giving the justice campaigner all the time in the world to move up and down the line, picking people off at will, telling me he 'got five years because of that bastard.' Behind me, a solicitor berated his secretary down his mobile phone, radiating anger and arrogance as he did so, ranting at her for 'not using her initiative' over sending a client some paperwork, his voice changing, like the worst sort of bully, to a pleading, wheedling tone when he rang the client to apologise, almost as if he was trying to stick his tongue down the phone line and onto the client's shoes, so desperate was he for the man's money, business and favour.

Slowly, we made it to the revolving doors. Inside, the staff were working as fast as they could, unable to cut any corners to get people in faster, the large numbers waiting the only reason things were slow. Then at last I was through the two scans and walking past the information desk, around to the left for the stairs. I left my bag in the now empty press room, most journalists already in court, then went up the last flight of stairs, across the carpeted waiting area, its rows of soft, comfy seats full of defendants and their families, and into Court 12.

Just as during the Shannon search, I had to find a new line for the story every day, and we were planning to fill the three front pages of the paper with our coverage of the trial. I was pleased that the story was being given the space and prominence it deserved, but also slightly concerned about finding enough strong material to fill all that space and wondering if all the most dramatic revelations had been made on the opening day. I needn't have worried; within the first ten minutes, the jury was hearing that when told that Shannon was safe, Karen had been more interested in the ringtone on a detective's mobile phone than in asking where her daughter had been found, or about her welfare.

Detective Constable Alex Grummitt, one of the family liaison officers working with the Matthews family, told the court that when he and colleague Mark Cruddace were driving Karen to Dewsbury Police Station to reunite her with Shannon, his mobile rang with a version of *Crazy*, the Gnarls Barkley song that spent several weeks at number 1 in 2006.

Karen liked the ringtone so much that she asked Detective Constable Grummitt to send it to her. 'I thought, We have just found your daughter,' he said in court. 'In my opinion it wasn't right.' He also revealed that on February 20, just a day after Shannon had been reported missing, Karen was equally taken with the 'quirky' ringtone on the mobile phone of another police officer. 'Karen Matthews' reaction was very unusual,' Detective Constable Grummitt said. 'She almost started dancing.'

He had also found Karen's response strange when he brought her the news everyone thought she had been desperate to hear: that her daughter had been found safe and well. 'It was a very unusual reaction. She hugged Craig and then she turned, I couldn't see her face. She turned away from me. Craig's eyes filled up and he appeared very emotional. She didn't ask any questions like "where have you found her?"'

More details about Karen's behaviour were given to the court by 'Scouse Pete' Brown's wife Natalie. She was around five feet tall, and only her head and shoulders were visible as she stood in the witness box, but she was confident, intelligent and highly articulate as she expanded on what Mr Goose had said the previous day. She described her former friend, Karen, as a 'Jekyll and Hyde' character who behaved one way in public and another in private. Craig, Karen and the children had stayed with the Browns while an extensive police search was made of number 24, and Natalie said that, in private, Karen behaved as if things were perfectly normal, helping her to clean the house and sharing a joke about everyday life. However, when the police were around, Karen would become quiet, upset and withdrawn.

Natalie also said that when a group of women from the Moor had been chatting amongst themselves at the TRA's community house, and one of them commented on a police officer's 'cute bum', Karen had chipped in that she wanted to 'take him upstairs'. When asked by Mr Goose, Natalie agreed that Karen had been laughing and joking behind closed doors.

However the key witness of that day was Detective Superintendent Andy Brennan, who had been handed the mammoth, daunting task of heading an inquiry into the little girl's disappearance. A six-footer, with short black hair and a prominent nose, Detective Superintendent Brennan is a softly spoken, thoughtful man, seemingly free of the laddishness of many CID men. He related in minute detail the scale of the search for Shannon, stating that the total cost of the inquiry had reached £3.2 million, 800 potential suspects had been interviewed, had their homes and vehicles searched and been required to provide a sample of their DNA, and that officers had followed leads, now known to be wild goose chases, as far from Dewsbury as Nottinghamshire and Cumbria.

Detective Superintendent Brennan said he started his shift at 7am on February 20. During the previous night, despite sub-zero temperatures, 200 officers had already been combing farmland and open areas, while Shannon's home and those of her friends were searched throughout the night. The number of policemen and women grew steadily, reaching nearly 400 at the height of the search, with 300 uniformed police, guided by a team of up to 85 detectives, more than four times the number usually put onto a murder case. They were headed by a group of about ten elite detectives, including Detective Superintendent Brennan himself. Those 95 detectives were all diverted from a string of serious crime inquiries, including murder and rape investigations.

Detective Superintendent Brennan explained that the search had initially been confined to within half-a-mile of 24 Moorside Road, because studies have shown that most abducted children are found within that distance of their home. His next revelation was a particularly chilling one: as early as the second day of the search, many detectives would already have been assuming that they were looking for a dead body; 'Ninety-six per cent of children have been found to be killed within twenty-four hours.'

CHAPTER 39

"TOBACCO BOUNTY" STORIES – in which a reward, in the prison currency of cigarettes, is claimed to be on offer to the first person to attack a particular prisoner – are regular fodder for the pages of the tabloids and are to be taken with a good pinch of salt. However, it is undeniable that high-profile prisoners and especially "nonces" - those accused of crimes against children - are prime targets for attack, often for no more reward than the kudos such an assault brings to the attacker. On the first Thursday of his trial, 13 November 2008, Mick Donovan was duly cornered by a fellow prisoner, who punched him twice, fracturing his jaw.

Mick would almost certainly have been targeted before that, but news of this attack spread beyond the walls of Armley Jail. His injuries left him unable to eat solid food and reduced to drinking soup or pureed food through a straw. On the following Monday, Mick sat in the dock, impassive and looking little different from normal, as his barrister, Alan Conrad, QC, told the court that Mick was in considerable pain, had not eaten properly for three days and was struggling to speak. As this would affect his ability to give evidence in his own defence, Mr Conrad applied for the trial to be suspended for one day so that his client could receive extra medical attention. His plea was granted by the judge, giving the jurors an unexpected day off and creating a security circus at the hospital where Mick was taken to for his treatment.

The press benches were rife with discussion over whether the trial would have to be further delayed, and if so, for how long, but early on Tuesday morning, word started to filter through that doctors had given Mick the all-clear and the case could continue. 'He's raring to go,' one veteran newsman said archly, as the familiar faces filed towards their seats. The public's appetite for the trial showed no sign of diminishing; the "public gallery full" sign had been placed on the door of Court 12 a full half-an-hour before the day's business was due to start.

The jury's first task of the day was to take a second look at the montage of television appeals for "help to find Shannon" that Karen had made. When it was shown on the first day of the trial, Karen had been unable to look at the screen and the footage left the courtroom stunned. Second time around, the effect was less dramatic, the silence not as pronounced, and Karen felt able to face her own image with one eye at least, the other still hidden behind a curtain of auburn hair. She kept her head slightly bowed as she watched herself, red-eyed and seemingly devastated, saying 'I am begging you baby, come home.'

Several more clips from GMTV, Look North, Calendar, BBC News and Sky News were shown one after another, followed by coverage from the pooled press conference in which Karen appeared to break down when asked what the last thing Shannon had said to her was. At that point, Karen finally turned her head away and stared straight ahead, down the courtroom, as the remaining footage was shown. The next clip showed one of the candlelit vigils, and finally there was footage of the day after Shannon had been found, with Karen giving a broad smile of apparently genuine relief. It seemed so real that, as I watched in that courtroom, I felt a small echo of the emotion and exultation I had felt on that day.

If the awed hush had been missing at the start of the montage, it had returned by the time Mr Goose nodded to his assistant to turn off the recording, and it was almost a relief when the first witness of the day took her place in the witness box. Carol Battye, a neighbour of Mick's, with strawberry blond hair and two gold hoops in each ear, told of a strange, late-night encounter with a woman she later identified as Karen, after spotting her near Mick's flat two days after Shannon vanished. She said she did not realise who Karen was at first, but, when talking to her daughter about the drama of the day Shannon was found, she described meeting the woman and her appearance, triggering a reply of 'Mum, you have just described Shannon's mother to me.'

Mrs Battye appeared slightly shy, but clearly did not suffer fools gladly, and did not seem to be intimidated by the cross examination by Karen's barrister, Frances Oldham QC, even though Mrs Battye was wrong-footed at least once over how heavily she had been exposed to Shannon's story through the papers and the television. In court she claimed that she only read The Daily Mirror for the crossword, but Mrs Oldham disputed that, citing evidence from Mrs Battye's police statement. The general consensus in the press-box was that the clash between those two formidable women, drawn from entirely different worlds, had ended as an honourable score-draw.

CHAPTER 40

PHYSICALLY, Detective Constable Paul Kettlewell looks like a stereotypical policeman: short-haired, powerfully built and speaking and carrying himself in that ultra-precise, straight-backed manner that coppers seem to grow into when they have spent years on the force. In dress-sense though, he was a long way from the sober-suited, stereotypical CID man. When he marched into Court 12 to give his evidence, he was decked out in designer spectacles, and an immaculately-pressed pinstriped suit, multi-coloured tie and a neatly-folded handkerchief in his breast pocket; all that and a goatee too. Perhaps it was fitting that such an unconventional tale of the discovery of a missing person should be related to the jury by such an unconventional looking police witness.

Detective Constable Kettlewell explained to the jury how he and his colleague, Detective Constable Nick Townsend, had been sent to Lidgate Gardens as part of the ongoing Shannon inquiry. After receiving no answer from Mick's flat, his suspicions were raised when he spoke to a neighbour, who pointed to the parked silver Peugeot car and said that Mick never went anywhere without it. Questioned by Mr Goose, the detective explained that he then called in an Operational Support Unit from Wakefield – an elite police search team trained and equipped to force its way into suspicious properties.

The search team took thirty-five minutes to assemble and make the ten-mile journey from Wakefield; for the two detective constables, waiting impatiently outside Mick's flat, that must have seemed like an age. When they arrived, they forced the locked door to Mick's home and another locked interior door. The policemen then all entered the silent and seemingly deserted flat. The officers carried out a search of the rooms, although the lack of sound made Detective Constable Kettlewell think that the place was empty. Suddenly he heard a girl's voice coming from a bedroom being searched by two of his colleagues. 'Stop it,' she said. 'You're frightening me.'

'I entered the room,' Detective Constable Kettlewell said. 'Two officers were standing by the bed. One of them turned towards me, and as I was beginning to think maybe the voice came from inside the bed, there was a noise as a small girl started to emerge from beneath it. PC Mosley and PC Greenwood helped the girl out and handed her to me. She was frightened and she was crying.'

Detective Constable Kettlewell said he recognised the girl as Shannon, and took her outside to a police car. Before arranging to take her to safety, he asked her where Mike was. Shannon replied that he was under the bed. 'I used my mobile phone to ring DC Townsend with that information,' he said.

PC Ian Mosley, a straightforward looking man who might be described as a "copper's copper," then took up the story. He described searching the bedroom, full of the stench of cigarette smoke. The bed, still warm to the touch, triggered questions in his mind, and felt strangely heavy when he tried to lift it. The two divans separated, with toys and clothes spilling out of one of them, and he heard a child's cry seeming to come from within the part of the bed he was lifting up.

Until then, the officer had been speaking in a low, monotone Yorkshire accent, but his astonishment at what he had seen was revealed in the way his voice went up an octave as he went on: 'It was quite surreal. As I heard the noise, Shannon started to pull herself out of the other side of the bed.' He then heard another noise, a light thump, which led him to look in the loft. PC Mosley said that he never found out what caused the thumping sound, and thought it was probably a noise from another flat, but in the loft he found the sinister elastic tether said to have been used to restrain Shannon. Before he could search the loft any further, PC Mosley heard a colleague shout, 'Stop resisting! Stop fighting!'

That colleague was PC Mathew Troake, a fresh-faced, young

copper, but already hardened by a couple of years working as a beat bobby, splitting up drunken fights on West Yorkshire streets, and kicking down doors with the Operational Support Unit. He gave his evidence confidently, and coped well with the hostile questioning of Mick's barrister, Alan Conrad QC. PC Troake said he was left alone in the bedroom where Shannon had been found, having walked in there just as she struggled out of the bed, and introduced herself by saying 'I'm Shannon'.

The other two officers then left the room, with PC Mosley searching the loft, but PC Troake said that he wanted to make sure the bedroom had been thoroughly searched, so he lifted the bed, found it was heavy, and went to the side the rescued girl had crawled out of. 'I looked into the hole,' he said, 'and saw a person I now know as Michael Donovan looking back at me. He was laid facing me in what I would describe as a foetal position. I immediately shouted at him to get out.'

PC Troake claimed that Mick refused to get out, and was cautioned and arrested on suspicion of abduction as he lay, still curled up, within his hiding place. PC Troake then picked the bed up, made the tiny entrance and exit hole bigger with his hands, and pulled Mick from the bed. He resisted, fighting and kicking, until colleagues arrived and helped to handcuff him. Even then, according to PC Troake, as Mick lay on the floor, wrists shackled, he still tried to sink his teeth into the hand of PC Matthew Haywood.

'We tried to take him down the stairs,' PC Troake said. 'He kept throwing himself against the wall, banging his head against the wall. As soon as we got him outside the house he refused to walk, we had to carry him. We took him to the waiting police van, he was put in the rear of the van where he said "Get Karen down here. We have got a plan, we're sharing the money, £50,000".'

The evidence given by PCs Haywood and Anthony Greenwood, the leader of the search team that day, was briefer, but almost as powerful as what had come before. PC Greenwood's appearance and body language were unusual for an officer giving evidence in court, in that he had stubble on his chin, his dress uniform looked slightly rumpled and he earned a ticking-off from Mr Conrad for having his hands in his pockets. PC Greenwood also looked moist-eyed when he closed his evidence, saying: 'It was the most surreal thing I have ever experience in my life . . . I am a parent myself, so the realisation that a little girl had been found, on that inquiry I had been working on for three weeks - there couldn't help but be some emotion.' It was a rare admission for any policeman, particularly a Yorkshire one, to make.

CHAPTER 41

AFTER A MULTI-MILLION POUND POLICE INQUIRY, one of the most painstaking and scientific ever carried out by West Yorkshire Police, Leeds Crown Court heard how the case was finally cracked by two straight-talking, full-time mums, former friends of Karen, who had turned their minds to a bit of amateur sleuthing. Natalie Brown and Julie Bushby had asked Karen to meet them, well away from the glare of the television cameras, to air the growing suspicions in their minds.

Detective Constable Christine Freeman, a police family liaison officer who had worked closely with Karen, agreed to drive her to the meeting point, a car park in Batley town centre, just down the road from the Moor but far enough away for them to be able to talk in private. When Julie and Natalie arrived, Karen and the police officer were already there, and they slid into the back seat.

The conversation began with Natalie bringing up the rumours that had been buzzing around the estate, rumours that both Mr Goose and the judge said they were not interested in hearing, since courts were a place for evidence, not gossip, chat or anecdote. Natalie, looking even smaller this time as she stood in the witness box, her hair in a ponytail, white blouse and dark trousers making her look like a teenager, told the court how she had confronted Karen with the theory she had formed: knowing that Karen wanted to leave Craig, Mick had offered her the chance to get away from Moorside Road, saying she could come and share his home at Batley Carr. He would already have picked Shannon up and she would be there waiting for her mum when she walked out on Craig and made her way to Lidgate Gardens.

However, Natalie suggested, the plan had gone wrong when Karen changed her mind about leaving Craig. She was then forced to improvise an explanation for Shannon's absence from Craig who,

Karen said in some evidence, had never laid a finger on her, but at another time claimed he had been violent towards her. 'She rang the police to cover the fact she was planning on leaving Craig,' Natalie said.

Mr Goose asked what Karen's reaction had been when Natalie put those thoughts to her. 'She said "Yes, it's true",' Natalie said. After that jaw-dropping revelation, Natalie and Julie seem to have kept remarkably composed, and continued to question Karen. When Natalie asked her to explain exactly what she meant by saying it was true, Karen claimed that she had been planning to leave Craig and wanted to take the children with her, but because Shannon had not turned up at the place where she was supposed to meet her mum, Karen had to go home where Craig was waiting, asking where his stepdaughter was.

By now, Natalie said, Karen was in floods of tears, shaking and scared, though Natalie described them as crocodile tears. On hearing this admission from a woman she had cared for and stood side-by-side with during the trauma of a child going missing, a flabbergasted Detective Constable Freeman got out of the car and rang her senior officer, who advised her to arrest Karen there and then on suspicion of abduction. When told she was being arrested, a sobbing Karen told her that she could not cope with going into a cell, but Detective Constable Freeman put her under caution and drove her to Dewsbury Police Station.

During the drive, as they tried to take in everything they had just heard, Julie and Natalie said that Karen was babbling. She claimed that she had only arranged for Mick to have Shannon for a couple of days, keeping her safe while she and Craig worked their way through some problems they had been having. She insisted she had not abducted her own daughter, asked what people on the estate would think of her, told Julie and Natalie that she had never had an affair with Mick, then made wild allegations, accusing Craig of being involved in Shannon's abduction, and that his mother, Alice, had something to do with it. She also claimed that she did not have Mick's phone number, had no way of contacting him and had never done so. Over and over, Karen made the same allegations: 'Craig had sorted it', 'Alice had sorted it', before, finally, confessing that she herself had 'sorted it'. She ended, Natalie said, by saying 'People will hate me for what I have done. I have disgraced my kids.'

Detective Constable Freeman took up the story of what happened when they arrived at Dewsbury Police Station. She took Karen inside to the custody suite, with Natalie and Julie going to another part of the police station to make statements. Karen was calmer now, Detective Constable Freeman said, her tears having dried up. The officer, who had spent so much time with Karen only to find out she had been the victim of a cruel deceit, still cared enough about Karen's feelings to ask for the custody suite to be cleared, saying she had worked with Karen for a long time and did not want to see her upset. However the desk sergeant said they couldn't clear the suite and in the end Detective Constable Freeman found a private area.

She said that Karen's tears returned when a detective explained the custody system to Karen. Now a suspect, not a victim, she began to speak, and though the detective wanted to wait for the formal interview, Karen would not be stopped. She accused Mick of abducting Shannon off his own bat, claimed people were putting words in her mouth, then twenty minutes later, she said she wasn't involved in the abduction, had only asked Mick to look after her daughter overnight, and didn't think he would keep her as long as he did.

Later, after being formally cautioned and charged, Karen claimed she did not know where her daughter was but knew who she was with. At the end of the formal interview, now a prisoner, Karen was placed in a police cell, the door clanging shut to leave her with four bare walls around her, a mattress and a toilet, no laces in her shoes, alone with the thoughts that must have been racing around in her head.

CHAPTER 42

MOST PEOPLE LOOKING TO GET AROUND A DRUG TEST, whether sporting cheats, or recreational users in a job where they are subject to random checks, know that the key is supplying a clean sample of urine. What is apparently less well known – not only by drug-takers, but even by those doing the testing, given the popularity of urine tests – is the long and detailed story that can be told by something that hangs around the body far longer than urine: hair.

It is extremely rare to hear audible intakes of breath in a courtroom, but when forensic toxicologist Craig Chatterton revealed that twenty month-old samples of Temazepam, and Melcozine, the active ingredient in Traveleeze, had been found in a twenty centimetre strand of Shannon's hair, Court 12 came close to a collective gasp of shock. Describing Temazepam as a 'potent hypnotic drug', Dr Chatterton said it would be unusual for children to be given it, such was its strength. Yet since that sample was taken in mid-March 2008, a twenty month history of Temazepam use meant that Shannon was being given the drugs as long ago as July 2006, when she was just seven years old.

At the conclusion of the expert evidence, the jury then heard statements taken from the two defendants, Karen's in interviews before and after she was arrested, and Mick's after his arrest. Had this been a routine trial, the statements might merely have been formal confirmation of much of the evidence that had already been aired in court, but almost nothing in this trial had been routine, and, true to form, these statements contained allegations that had not been aired in court until that moment, including Karen's wild claim that she thought her parents were involved with Shannon's abduction, the grave allegations she made against Craig, including a repeat of the accusation that he had been violent towards her, and a claim that Craig had planned the whole escapade to make Karen appear an unfit mother.

The statements were read to the court by Detective Constable John Lee, a mountain of a man, with a black moustache and the seemingly obligatory "copper's crop" hairstyle. Reading Karen's words, he described the normal routine at 24 Moorside Road, on the day Shannon went missing. Karen said her alarm went off at 7am, when she got up to wake Shannon and her brother, the two of them not wanting to get up, but eventually managing it. Karen gave them breakfast, dressed them and took them to school, before returning for two of the younger children. After dropping them off, she went back home to watch television: The Jeremy Kyle Show, one of her favourites. Ryan came round to play on the X-box, while Karen browsed Ebay, and watched some more television until it was time to go and pick up the kids.

Before Detective Constable Lee read Mick's statements, one more witness was squeezed in, Mick's former employer, Colin Backhouse, who gave the jury a clearer picture of Mick's character, or at least what he was like in the early 1990s, when he was employed at BBM Engineering. Although brief, Mr Backhouse's appearance, was a welcome moment of light relief towards the end of a long day, both because of his dress sense - moleskin jacket, pink and yellow spotted tie and immaculate brown loafers - which, while not as striking as that of Detective Constable Kettlewell, still stood out, and his air of an accomplished joke-teller or after-dinner speaker, projecting his evidence across the court in loud, clear, broad, West Yorkshire tones.

Mr Backhouse said he had employed Mick as a driver and labourer in 1989. His employee, who was then just nineteen, loved to get behind the wheel, 'driving was his life,' as Mr Backhouse put it, but Mick's naivety and lack of common sense, led his boss to take him under his wing, 'He used to get a bit agitated about taking the delivery out, and he was getting on my nerves, so I gave him £20 and told him to put diesel in the pick-up. I looked out of the window and saw him drive past, then going back the other way. When he came back and I asked him what he was up to, he said there had only been room in the tank for £18.40 worth of diesel, so he was driving around to use some up so he could get the other £1.60 in. He was one for looking after.' That story prompted one of the loudest peals of laughter I have ever heard in a courtroom.

Despite the joke, Mr Backhouse was clearly sympathetic to Mick's problems and limitations and said that when he became concerned at Mick's apparent lack of interest in food, he gave him money to buy lunch, only to see his young employee returning to work having spent it on 100 penny bubblegums. At that point his boss stopped giving him money and started bringing in extra sandwiches for him instead. He also told a story that showed how dedicated to his work and eager to please his young employee had been. Mick had crashed the pick-up while on his way back to the engineering works from making a collection and was taken to Leeds General Infirmary for treatment. Mr Backhouse was then contacted by medical staff saying Mick had named him as his next-of-kin.

'When I got there he reached into the bed and pulled out a package, saying "I've got the job you wanted Colin".'

CHAPTER 43

NEARLY 400 POLICEMEN, almost a quarter of them the elite CID, searching for a little girl and swarming all over the area surrounding her home, and yet the man holding her is able to take her to the shops and to the park. It sounds a fantastic claim, but was made by Mick in his statements to police and later read at his trial.

According to those statements, Mick took Shannon to the supermarket twice, once to Tesco in Batley, when it was dark, the other time to Asda in Dewsbury, to parks in Batley and Birstall three times, and on another occasion for a ride in his car to give her a break from the flat and some fresh air. While on those trips, Shannon sat in the back of the car in her pink coat with the hood up. Mick also claimed that she liked living with him, finding him kind and generous, unlike her parents.

He also said that Shannon saw no news bulletins or newspapers, during the 24 days she was at his flat and had no idea people were looking for her, and claimed that Craig and Karen were so much in debt that they might have been facing a visit from the bailiffs. Those statements, once more read in court by Detective Constable Lee, should have paved the way for Mick to enter the witness box and give evidence in his own words, but, still suffering from the injuries sustained in the prison assault, he had to wait slightly longer for his day in court.

Exactly a week after the first postponement for Mick to receive medical attention, everyone who trooped into Court 12 found themselves being sent home again, this time because Mick was now in recovery after emergency surgery on his jaw, having been rushed from his prison cell to hospital two days earlier. Explaining the postponement, the judge told the jury: 'Mr Donovan is in rather a bad way. Just before the weekend, we heard the medical opinion was that he had to have immediate surgery. We are in the hands of the doctors,

I'm afraid.'

That less-than-hopeful remark triggered another bout of feverish rumour in the press ranks about whether the trial could continue, and how long it would be delayed but in the event, it went ahead the next morning. As we assembled in court, just before 10.30am, we heard the two abrupt raps on the door that warn those present to get to their feet, and quickly. The door swung open, to reveal not one, but two men, as walking in behind the judge was a grey-haired man in his 50s, wearing a crushed velvet tunic with white lace cuffs and a white lace ruff around his neck, and carrying a long, curved sword in his hand. He looked like Black Rod, the man seen once a year at the state opening of parliament, but was introduced by the judge as 'the High Sheriff of West Yorkshire, like all his predecessors, he takes an interest in the administration of justice.'

The two pillars of the establishment took their seats and Mr Goose formally declared the prosecution's case complete. His counterpart, Mr Conrad, then called on Mick to enter the witness box and give his evidence. The dock officer unlocked the gate and gestured to Mick, who was dressed in blue jeans, blue and white canvas trainers and a navy sweatshirt, to walk the six feet or so from the dock to the witness box. As Mick did so, he looked more like a broken man in his seventies than someone in his forties. His complexion was ghost-white, and the corners of his mouth seemed permanently turned down. As he walked past the press benches, his stooping, frail figure, looked even smaller than his five foot eight inches. His steps were slow and hesitant, as if afraid to leave a safe and secure refuge, locked in the dock and flanked by prison guards, for the exposed, alien territory of the open courtroom.

Much of the chatter in the press room beforehand had been whether reporters, lawyers, and, more importantly, the jury, would be able to hear Mick at all when he took the stand, so quiet had been the few words he had uttered in open court up to that point. As he got into the box, and was asked to take the oath and identify himself, his voice was little more than a whisper, and barely audible on the press benches, let alone to the jurors, who were a little further away. There was a pause as action was taken to increase the volume, with an usher piling up books, one of them The Bible, to raise the microphone closer to his mouth.

Mr Conrad first asked his client about his past criminal record, and the court heard that he had convictions for arson as a twelve year-old, which landed him a spell at an attendance centre, with other convictions for shoplifting, criminal damage, and trying to obtain property, namely medicine, by deception. In the present context, however, the most significant revelation about Mick's previous contacts with the law, came about something that did not end in a conviction: the time when he was charged with abducting one of his own daughters. Charges were brought, but later dropped.

Mick also revealed more detail about his background, saying he had gone to a "special school" because of difficulties in reading, writing and 'understanding things in life', but that he was bullied there, and left at sixteen to work in a job his dad got for him, in a trouser pressing factory. His learning difficulties made it a challenge for him to master The Highway Code and get his driving licence; it took more than 100 lessons and two driving tests before he succeeded.

He also revealed a liking for action heroes, and said that Mike Donovan, leading man in the science fiction series "V", rather than Jason Donovan, was the inspiration for his name change, made because of the unhappy connotations of his real name, Paul Drake, ammunition for the bullies who had tormented him at school and who he still saw around town as a young man. 'They used to pick on me and call me names,' he said.

Mick said he had first met Karen when she and Craig visited his flat a couple of times, months before the Shannon saga. He claimed he didn't like her and was scared of her because she kept threatening him. He said that he had seen her again at the funeral wake for Brian

Meehan, Craig's dad, held at a pub on Heckmondwike Road, Dewsbury, in December 2007. Contradicting evidence given earlier by the pub's then-landlord, Mick claimed that he had not gone into the pub, but had stayed outside, and was having a smoke on the balcony, when Karen came out to do the same. They did not speak but Karen, as Mick put it, was 'looking straight at me.'

'How did you feel when she looked at you?' Mr Conrad asked.

'I didn't really like it,' Mick said. He claimed that he next saw Karen a month later, when she and Craig were shouting and swearing at each other in the street, then again, a short time afterwards, when she flagged him down in his car, and asked him to meet her at a café where, he claimed, she bullied him into taking part in the Shannon plan, threatening him that if he didn't do as she said, 'three lads' would 'come and do my car in, my flat in and me in.' He also said that when she flagged him down, she asked him for a loan of £20,000, but he told her he did not have that sort of money, and would not have lent it even if he had.

By now, Mick was dealing with the questions reasonably confidently, thinking for half-a-beat before answering but giving a similar version of events to the one he had told the police in his prepared statements. His voice was now more audible, with a hint of a Yorkshire accent, as well as some childlike pronunciations, like 'threckend' for 'threatened' and 'hospical' for 'hospital'; he also made the common mistake of calling Shannon 'Sharon'. A few feet away, Karen cut an isolated figure as, arms folded, she watched and listened from the dock, the one remaining officer sitting well away from the defendant he was guarding.

Mick then told the jury that the day after he had met Karen in the café, and had received the supposed threats, his car was broken into outside his flat, his SatNav system stolen from his glove box, and he thought he had seen a youth running away from the scene. He chose not to report the incident to the police, got the window fixed and the next day drove to visit his sister, Alice. He said he saw Karen in the street again, and that she pushed a pram in front of his car to make him stop, then leaned in through the open window and said, 'I see you've got your window fixed.' When Mick asked how she knew about it, he claimed that Karen replied, 'Remember the plan or else they will come and burn your car out.'

Mick said he felt he had to do as he was told, and picked Shannon up at about 4pm on February 19. She was excited, having been told by her mum that she was going to a fair, but Mick said it was too foggy for the fair, and they went to his flat instead, where Shannon was 'calm and relaxed'.

Mick said that Karen called him the next day from Alice's phone, but declined to speak to her daughter, saying, 'No, we have to keep it short. Stick to the plan.' He claimed that when he pointed out that Shannon had no extra clothes or any toys with her, Karen just said, 'You've got money, go and buy them.' He then went out to buy clothes and food - Shannon's favourite pizzas and takeaways - and the two ate them and watched DVDs together, and Mick claimed that Shannon told him she was better looked after at his flat than at number 24, where there were too many arguments and too much drinking, and where Craig had once thrown a can of lager at his stepdaughter's head.

Mr Conrad also asked his client about the list of "do's and don'ts" for Shannon, rules that Mick claimed he had taken from a page of instructions Karen gave him when they met at the café. However, he said that the elastic tether in the attic was a complete surprise to him, and that he had never seen it before. He said that he had never even been in the loft, and suggested that builders might have left the tether there. He also claimed that he had never drugged Shannon, saying that his Temazepam had been in the living room and that she might have helped herself to it.

Mick's testimony had lasted only half a day, an unusually short time for a defendant, but Mr Conrad asked no further questions, leaving Mick to face the far less sympathetic approach of Mrs

Oldham and Mr Goose. Mrs Oldham began fairly slowly, establishing Mick as someone who, in his life, had experienced no difficulties in caring for himself, managing his finances and benefits, and buying and maintaining cars. She then raised the statement from his sister, Maria Harper, in which she had described her brother as a storyteller and a fantasist.

Under Mrs Oldham's questioning, it wasn't long before Mick's apparent confidence faded and his voice dropped until it was again barely audible. Mrs Oldham asked him to speak up and even moved her own position so the jury had a clear view of him, then stepped up the pace, asking why, if he was so scared of Karen, he had not been pleased when the police arrived at his flat as his liberators. She then pressed him on who had made the hole in his bed. Mick denied it had been him but floundered as he did so, and Mrs Oldham also exposed inconsistencies in his evidence about whether he had been inside the pub at Brian Meehan's wake. She quickly teased out another one, with Mick changing his story about where Karen had asked him for £20,000. He corrected Mrs Oldham when she said it was in the café, claiming it was in his car, then switched back to the café. Mick was struggling, but was literally saved by the bell - for the moment at least – when the court's fire alarm went off, forcing an evacuation of the building and an end to the proceedings for the day.

CHAPTER 44

BEING CROSS-EXAMINED BY GEORGE CARMAN, the late and legendary QC, was once described as like walking down a lonely country lane, high hedges at either side, as one-by-one the gates slammed shut, the only route remaining straight into a dead end. Carman was a one-off, but a grilling by even the weakest of barristers can be a tough and unsettling experience. When court resumed the next morning, with a simple-minded man like Michael Donovan as prey, Mrs Oldham and Mr Goose soon had him squirming. He had been saved by the fire alarm's bell the previous day, but it was only a temporary stay of execution, and now he was back in the witness box, facing Mrs Oldham's stern gaze, as she looked at him over the top of her bi-focal spectacles.

Mrs Oldham, representing Karen, first implied that Mick had sought to replace his estranged daughter with Shannon, by dressing her in his daughter's clothes, getting her to write letters to his daughter and to draw a picture of Blackpool, the place Mick had taken his offspring on his failed abduction attempt in 2006. 'Did you regard her (Shannon) as being like your daughter?' Mrs Oldham asked. Mick denied it, but later Mrs Oldham reminded him of that Blackpool trip, when he had signed into the B&B under a false name, and put to him that on March 13, the day before Shannon was found, he had told a pharmacist he was going to Blackpool for the weekend.

The barrister also took Mick through the wording of a strange letter police found in his flat, addressed to someone called John, which talked about what Shannon and her dad were going to do when they went to Blackpool, and was signed off 'love Shannon and dad.' Mick insisted Shannon had written the letter and drawn the picture of her own free will, and that the dad she referred to was Craig Meehan.

A short woman, but a formidable one, speaking in deep, commanding tones, Mrs Oldham then alleged that the plan to snatch and hide Shannon involved Mick and other members of his extended family, and that Karen was not one of the plotters. Mrs Oldham said Mick was the person controlling the plan, telling him: 'Mr Donovan, you knew exactly what you were doing, didn't you? You were the one in control, you were in control of Shannon?' His voice once more an almost inaudible whisper, so that the judge constantly had to ask him to speak up, Mick barely seemed to deny Mrs Oldham's allegations.

As he had walked to the witness box that morning, his gait had been easier, and he appeared much more confident, but he quickly retreated into himself, prompting Mr Goose to comment that, 'The jury may think you have presented yourself as a quietly spoken man, a rather fragile man, weak, rather helpless.' Mick agreed with this, but Mr Goose's remarks were not made out of sympathy, and he then asked for the montage of CCTV footage of Mick on shopping trips in Dewsbury and Batley, to be played to the jury again.

In contrast to the opening day, when the clips were allowed to run through, one after another, the film was paused frequently while Mr Goose asked the jury to compare Mick's seemingly confident, straight-backed walking style on the screen to the stooped figure that had shuffled from the dock to the witness box as he went to give evidence for the first time. He also asked the jury to observe how, despite Mick's claim that he was taking part in the plot out of fear, he never showed any signs of being worried that someone might be watching or following him. He also rejected Mick's claims that he had taken Shannon out on shopping trips and to parks, putting to him that she had been kept locked in the flat throughout the entire 24 days. While the CCTV was being shown, Mick told the jury that Shannon had been out shopping with him at least four times - twice the number he had claimed in his prepared police statements read to the court earlier in the trial.

Mr Goose also confronted Mick about the long leather strap, which he was alleged to have used to restrain Shannon while he was out on his shopping trips. 'I suggest it was used by you in order to enforce your control of Shannon in the flat, particularly when you left her alone. Is it just a coincidence that the strap, when pulled down, wouldn't permit somebody who has it wrapped round them from leaving the flat?' Mick's response was to deny any knowledge of the strap, in the roof-space of the flat where he had lived for four years. 'I don't know anything about the strap,' he said.

Following Mrs Oldham's lead at the start of her questioning, Mr Goose also sought to establish Mick as someone capable of thinking and acting for himself, managing his finances, living alone, buying, selling and maintaining cars, a person far from the vulnerable, damaged looking creature who gave confused, whispered, one-word answers to seemingly straightforward questions. As the cross-examination continued, the judge kept reminding Mick to speak up, showing his frustration as he said, 'Come on, Mr Donovan, we know you can speak louder than this.'

Later in the day, the defence team countered the prosecution's efforts to present Mick as a capable, independent figure, by calling an expert witness: Dr David Glasgow, a forensic and clinical psychologist. Dr Glasgow described Mick as a highly impressionable figure who suffered from severe mental health problems. He was of limited intelligence and suffered from serious emotional issues, the doctor said, and psychometric tests had found his patient had memory problems, a long history of depression, and an IQ on the border between learning difficulties and a more severe learning disability.

CHAPTER 45

DAY 16 OF THE TRIAL WAS SUPPOSED TO BE KAREN'S DAY, the eagerly awaited moment when she would appear in the witness box, but a bizarre rumour, which began circulating the previous afternoon, suggested that she might yet be upstaged by her former partner. Craig Meehan, so the rumours went, had decided to come and watch his ex-partner giving evidence. Concerned about the chaos his arrival would cause amongst the press camped outside the court, the police had laid on a car to bring him in and then take him home again. The source of the rumour was unknown, but it was taken pretty seriously until the following morning when a well-connected television reporter was able to confirm that Craig would definitely be elsewhere that day.

That minor commotion over, the focus switched firmly back to Karen, and the "will she/won't she" debate over whether or not she would give evidence in her own defence. Reporters with some legal experience said that given the weight of the case against her, she would be mad to put herself into the sights of elite lawyers such as Messrs Conrad and Goose, but, from my own knowledge of Karen's character, I fancied that she would be in no mood to be told what she could and couldn't do.

That view was backed up by one experienced police officer who had worked on the Shannon case throughout. 'It'll be a case of "I know best" with Karen,' he said. 'No one can tell her anything. She will think she is in the right, everyone else is wrong, and if she gets stuck, she'll just lie.'

As it had been every day, the public gallery was packed, though on this morning a strange smell of chip fat was rising from the clothes of someone sitting there. The day's business began with evidence from two expert witnesses, Dr Glasgow completing his testimony, then Dr Harry Wood, another psychologist, called to give his. The fire alarm again went off when he had barely started his evidence, and the crowd of lawyers, journalists, defendants, court staff and spectators milled about outside, in the damp and cold, with the journalists in particular getting itchy over the lost time while the firefighters turned up to confirm the false alarm. An hour's business was lost, before Dr Wood completed his evidence, reaching broadly similar conclusions to his colleague about Mick's mental state.

The lunch-break was then called, but anticipation started to build as a senior lawyer told us to 'expect the star turn after lunch'. Karen duly took the stand, but only after an unusual address to the jury by her QC, Mrs Oldham. Her message to the seven men and five women was that despite everything they had seen or read, they should not pre-judge Karen and anything she had to say. Mrs Oldham claimed that the media and the police had convicted Karen before the trial had even begun, highlighting the fact that some officers had given television interviews, to be broadcast after the trial. 'How many of us have watched news reports in which a tearful appeal is made for the safe return of a family member or loved one?' she said. 'How many of us have decided that he or she is responsible? In our modern age it is almost a cliché. That is what has happened in this case. The media and the police have decided that Karen Matthews is guilty. The important thing to remember is this: there are only twelve people in this country who have the opportunity of considering not just smear, not just prejudice, but of hearing the evidence in this case.'

With that, Karen was called to give her evidence. She looked a little uneasy as she rose from the seat in the dock that she had occupied for more than two weeks. Her jacket buttoned up to the neck, she walked slowly, ponderously, to the witness box. She hitched up her jeans before taking the oath, her features hidden from the press benches and public gallery by her thick curtain of red hair, and her words still stunted but sounding less harsh, more childlike, than they had done on the streets of Dewsbury Moor.

Karen's first questioner was her own barrister, Mrs Oldham, a friendly face, giving her the opportunity to deny having anything to do with Shannon's disappearance, or any threats that were made to Mick, to force him to take part in the plan. After just half-a-dozen questions, Mrs Oldham asked her client what her reaction had been when she learned that Shannon had been less than a mile away from home throughout the entire 24 days. Karen claimed that the first she knew of the place where her daughter had been held was when she saw pictures of it on the television news. As she spoke, the first tears started to pour from her eyes, those eyes that the world had seen cry, but that the jury had heard would be wet for the cameras and dry for friends.

It appeared that Karen had been coached in her answers, replying 'I did not,' rather than 'no,' to the questions about her involvement - words her former friends said she would never normally use. The tears started to flow more freely when Mrs Oldham asked Karen about her relationship with Craig. Her voice started to tremble as she claimed that she was scared she of him, and made serious allegations against him, repeating her claims that he could be violent, abusive and aggressive towards her, saying that he would call her, 'fat and ugly'. She also claimed that he would be verbally abusive to one of her children, though, strangely, she insisted that he had never acted that way towards Shannon

Karen told the jury that she had met Mick at the pub where Craig's father's wake was being held, but that they had only said 'Hello'. They met again a few hours later at Alice Meehan's house, where Karen said she had fled after Craig had become drunk and abusive, because only his mother knew how to calm him down. She claimed Mick had offered her and the children a place to stay, she turned him down because she wanted to sort out her problems with Craig, and said Mick 'looked disgusted because I did not take up his offer.'

Mrs Oldham then asked Karen if she had any knowledge of the drugs, including Temazepam, found in Shannon's hair samples. In her eagerness to deny it, Karen jumped in with her standard 'I did not' response before Mrs Oldham had even finished asking her the question. Mrs Oldham then asked her client about Shannon's schooling, presumably so that Karen could tell the jury there had been no complaints from teachers about Shannon appearing drowsy or dozy, but Karen fluffed her lines, and looked flustered and embarrassed when she had to admit that she had no idea which school year her daughter was in. The QC paused for a second and the silence in the courtroom was electric, unbroken even by a cough or a sniff, everyone engrossed in the exchanges between lawyer and client.

Karen described the day Shannon had gone missing, and then the court heard again the tape of the 999 call she made to the police. This time Karen had to listen to it from the raised, exposed point of the witness box, rather than from behind the Perspex shields of the dock. 'Were you play-acting then, Miss Matthews?' Mrs Oldham asked.

'I was not.'

'How did you feel making that call?'

'Upset,' Karen said, and then the tears and sobs took over again and the judge called for a recess before Karen began the ordeal of cross-examination, from barristers who would be much less gentle and sympathetic than Mrs Oldham.

When the trial resumed, Mr Conrad rose to begin the cross-examination. His questions were slow and deliberate at first as he probed Karen's claim that Craig had planned the whole escapade. Mr Conrad asked her why, if Craig really planned it, she had not contacted the police about it, and rode roughshod over her claims that she was scared of Craig. Mr Conrad accused her of living a lie and being an accomplished liar, and asked her whether her account of events had always been the same, well knowing the answer, but wanting to hear what Karen would tell the jury. Her carefully worded reply was that 'I have always said I have never had anything to do with it.'

Mr Conrad pressed Karen again and again over the changes and inconsistencies in her story, varying his pace, facial expressions and body language, and raising and lowering his voice - the barrister as actor, the courtroom his stage. The other player in this drama repeatedly fluffed her lines or forgot those she had already delivered, giving her interrogator more ammunition to throw back at her.

Karen had continued to cry throughout this interrogation, sometimes sniffling, at other times with tears flowing freely, but about half-way through her questioning by Mr Conrad she seemed to regain some composure, and began to give audible answers rather than simply saying 'No' or not replying at all. She told the barrister she had been disgusted to hear that Shannon had been found at Mick's flat, as he was family, and said 'No, I did not' when Mr Conrad said she had known where her daughter had been all along, and denied his suggestion that underneath the tears and emotion she was 'a hard woman really, a manipulative woman, a woman who uses people.'

Karen's self-control was tested when Mr Conrad confronted her with the forensic evidence about her daughter's prolonged use of Temazepam, extending back well over a year before her kidnap. The barrister then turned the screw again, 'You know the difference between telling the truth and telling a lie,' he said. 'You lied to the police, didn't you?'

When Karen denied it, Mr Conrad said 'You are even lying about that now. You gave different accounts in your interviews with the police, didn't you?'

When Karen claimed she did so because she was scared, Mr Conrad then produced transcripts of the interviews and went on to tie her in knots over the inconsistencies they contained. Those interviews, given to police in February and March, must have seemed to Karen to have come from a different epoch. Back then, she was the apparently helpless victim of a terrible crime, an object of sympathy and compassion. Now she stood accused of being the perpetrator of that crime, a pariah spurned by her former friends, hounded by the press, and skewered by the questions of a relentless, hostile QC, doing his job and doing it well.

Mr Conrad still had more to say to her, but the judge called a halt at 4.15pm. Karen could return to the cells for now, but her interrogator would again be waiting to greet her in the morning. She walked back to the dock, heaving a sigh, her eyes puffy and red, and her heavily made-up face streaked with the tracks of the tears she had shed. Whether they were genuine or crocodile tears was something that the jurors would have to decide.

CHAPTER 46

HER EYELIDS HEAVY WITH SMUDGED MAKE-UP, Karen strode purposefully out of the dock on her second day in the witness box, her back straight and a grim expression on her face, as though determined to erase the memory of the previous afternoon's ordeal from her mind and give a better account of herself this time. A new day and a fresh mind might make her second encounter with the hostile QCs less harrowing than the first.

If so, her hopes were soon dashed. Precisely seven minutes after Mr Conrad asked his first question of the day, which Karen answered in her small, childlike voice, she was back in floods of tears. The opening barrage of questions was aimed at casting doubt on Karen's claims that she was being controlled by Craig, who had been the ringleader of the whole plot, and had threatened her with violence if she did not tell the police she had asked Mick to take Shannon. According to this version of events, Craig had told her to act as a frontwoman because, if she was caught, as a woman with no criminal record, she would be treated more lightly.

Mr Conrad raised the point that Karen had been in other relationships, and had not been scared to leave those men, so why should she be scared to leave Craig? Holding her own reasonably well at first, Karen countered that all the other men had left her. When she repeated her claim that she had played no part in the kidnap plot, Mr Conrad accused her of telling blatant lies and pointed to the contradictions in her statements to the police. Karen tried to explain those away by saying she was confused during the police interviews and did not know what she was saying, but Mr Conrad fired back that she had had the benefit of a solicitor throughout the interviews, and the opportunity of regular breaks to compose herself, had she wanted them.

Karen's response was that she had just wanted to get the interviews over and done with, and at this stage her voice was still quiet and her eyes dry. Next, though, Mr Conrad produced a newspaper photograph of Karen and Craig publicising the search for Shannon. At once the floodgates opened, the tears started pouring down Karen's face as she claimed she had not wanted to pose for the picture, that Craig had made her do it. That made me raise my eyebrows, as it looked like a picture taken while I had actually been with Craig and Karen, and I hadn't seen Craig apply any pressure on her to take part.

Mr Conrad then asked Karen why, if she was really frightened of Craig, she had not asked officers for help to save her from her violent partner when she was in the safety of a police station, giving interviews. Karen managed some sort of answer but then made another new claim that the court had not heard before, saying that she had believed Shannon was at her brother's house. Her answers were now becoming more and more hesitant with longer and longer silences after Mr Conrad's questions, until, with more than a hint of impatience in his voice, the judge said, 'Answer the question, Miss Matthews.'

Karen composed herself briefly, the tears stopped and there was a harder edge to her voice as she tried to counter Mr Conrad's questions, but she was again floundering as he explored Karen's scarcely credible claim in a police interview, that though she knew Shannon was with Mick, she didn't know where Mick lived, and had no way of getting hold of him. When the police asked why she did not go through Alice, Mick's sister, Karen said that she couldn't get hold of Alice and did not have her number, despite the fact she shared a house with Alice's son, lived just two minutes walk from her and next-door to her daughter.

Mr Conrad had only questioned Karen for half-an-hour that morning, but that had been time enough to tie her in as many knots as the previous afternoon. He finished his cross-examination by teasing from her the admission that she had gone to collect a SatNav system before ringing 999 to report Shannon missing, and had then done a supermarket shop after she had made the call. She claimed that she needed food for her other children, but the admission that this allegedly distraught mother had had time for a shopping expedition on the night her daughter disappeared, had a visible impact on the jury.

There was to be no let-up for Karen, as the counsel for the prosecution, Mr Goose, rose slowly to his feet. He began his questioning in slow, velvety, almost gentle, tones, asking Karen if there had been any discussion of the reward money on offer and what could be done with it. When Karen said that there had been, the barrister pounced, asking why she would be involved in such discussions - surely a traumatised mother's only priority would be to get her daughter home? Karen insisted that she had never wanted any of the money, and the barrister then switched the focus of his attack, using Karen's frequent changes of story against her. As he asked her if she had taught her children that it is wrong to lie, that liars get caught out and get into trouble, he almost sounded like a parent ticking off a naughty child.

Mr Goose then told Karen that, so far, she had given five different versions of her involvement with the circumstances that led to Shannon being at Mick's Lidgate Gardens flat. Her tears returned, but, whereas Mr Conrad had chosen to ignore them, Mr Goose asked, 'Why are you crying, Miss Matthews?'

'Because I am getting blamed for something I haven't done.'

The QC then asked if the tears were because Karen was feeling sorry for herself, that she had got herself into a predicament and could see no way out of it. Karen's replies often failed to answer the question put to her, but she continued to insist she had not been involved in the abduction, at one point adding, 'I love my kids to bits.' However, there was malice in her voice as she said that some of the neighbours who helped with the search for Shannon had never been close to the Matthews clan, and had only got involved when the child went missing. It struck me as petty, spiteful, over-the-garden-wall dispute stuff, that would do her no favours with the jury.

Mr Goose's voice no longer had its soothing, velvet tone, and he sounded more sarcastic and disbelieving with every new sentence, and the longer the cross-examination went on, the more Karen seemed to sink into herself, her voice dropping lower and lower and her body hunching as if she was trying to make herself as small a target as possible. 'She's close to cracking,' one senior journalist whispered, as she sat behind me on the press benches.

Karen didn't crack, but she continued to dig deeper and deeper holes for herself, denying that she had admitted that she knew where Shannon was during the showdown with Julie Bushby and Natalie Brown in the car, even though the admission had been witnessed by Detective Constable Freeman, who felt that she was left with no choice but to arrest her. All three women had independently told the court, under oath, of Karen's admission, yet still she denied that she had made it.

'Are you someone who will say just about anything that you think to try and wriggle out of the obvious?' Mr Goose asked, before showing Karen the statements from the encounter in the car. She claimed to have been confused, but when Mr Goose asked what she had been confused about, his question led to a long, uncomfortable period of silence. As the lawyer waited for an answer, Karen, hiding behind her hair, was seemingly reduced to hoping he would go away. Mr Goose kept trying to peer behind the veil of red-hair, to make eye-contact with her and kept repeating 'What?', until Karen eventually blurted out, with some defiance: 'It felt like everyone was blaming me for something that I had not done.'

After about an hour in the box, with Mr Goose still pressing her over the many changes in her story, Karen was in tears again, and when the judge offered her a ten-minute adjournment, she accepted with alacrity, scuttling back to the anonymity of the dock, head down, as soon as the judge gave her permission to do so.

After the break, Karen was again confronted with her television appeals for Shannon's safe return, with Mr Goose trying to undermine her claims that Craig had controlled her and threatened her, by pointing out how close the couple appeared in some of the footage, with Karen describing her partner as 'her rock'. Footage was shown of Craig with his arm around Karen's shoulders and the couple sharing a kiss after Shannon had been found. At this point the court clerk had to bring Karen a fresh box of tissues, so many tears had she shed that day.

Mr Goose drew his cross-examination to a close by putting to Karen that she knew the plot was all about money. Karen answered that she 'did not know Donovan had her'. Mr Goose replied: 'I suggest you are lying about that, as you have lied time and time again,' before sitting down without another glance at his quarry. Released from the witness box, Karen returned to the dock with a sullen look on her face, and the judge then adjourned the hearing for lunch.

The rumour that Craig might yet put in an appearance was still buzzing about, like a fly trapped in the windowless court complex, and during the lunch-break, at least two reporters strode breathlessly into the press room to declare that they had been told on good authority that he was here, and was likely to be giving evidence in Karen's defence, despite all the allegations she had made against him. 'He is definitely here,' one said. 'He was brought into the building with a blanket over his head.'

As on the previous day, if Craig really was there, he was keeping an extremely low profile, and had not been called to give evidence in his former partner's defence. Instead, a delivery driver called Mark Goode appeared, a thickset, shaven-headed man with a broad West Yorkshire accent, who addressed the judge as 'Your Honour' and clearly and confidently explained how he had been delivering a bed to a Dewsbury Moor address at about 5.30pm on March 14, 2008, when the celebrations that Shannon had been found were just beginning.

Mr Goode said he had walked into the house, where pictures of Lidgate Gardens were being shown on the television, and that he had commented to the woman householder, 'I would burn that bastard,' meaning Donovan. The woman replied, 'That is a family member.'

Mr Goode's response, he said, was 'Never!' He said the woman was standing near the fireplace, in his words, 'panicking'. He went to get the base of the bed, and claiming that when he came back, he heard the woman speaking on the telephone. 'I didn't know who she was,' he told the court, 'I thought she was an everyday customer, but she looked like she was shitting herself. I heard her say "Don't say nowt. Just keep your mouth shut. They will never find out."' Mr Goode said he later learned that the woman he had delivered the bed to was Alice Meehan.

With that, Mrs Oldham said simply: 'My Lord, that was the case for Karen Matthews.' The case was adjourned for the weekend but, in a saga approaching the ten-month mark, the endgame was now in sight.

CHAPTER 47

IT WAS FITTING that the final acts in the near-ten month Shannon Matthews' saga should be played out in similarly freezing temperatures to those that gripped Dewsbury Moor during the 24 days that Shannon was missing. As the queues formed outside Leeds Crown Court, waiting to hear the barristers make their closing speeches to the jury, there was ice on the pavements, and a thin dusting of snow on windowsills, car roofs and the tops of bus shelters. The people waiting outside the entrance to the court, blew on their hands, stamped their feet and hunched their shoulders, trying to ward off the biting cold.

Mrs Oldham, Karen's barrister, was just ahead of me as we passed through security, immaculate in an olive-green, ankle length overcoat, black patent leather shoes and matching handbag. Her off-duty bright smile and relaxed banter with the guards were in marked contrast to the ultra-professional, almost fierce figure she presented in the courtroom.

Once through the metal-detectors, Mrs Oldham swept through the foyer to the robing room, the barrister's equivalent of the actor's dressing room, to prepare for a pivotal day for her client. A few minutes later, she took her place in court, the smile replaced by a frown of concentration as she read through some papers, pausing now and again to talk to a colleague, in a low voice. Mr Goose sifted through a pile of documents and leafed through a weighty legal tome, while his junior counsel, Simon Kealey, tapped away on a laptop keyboard.

The press benches were the quietest they had been since the start of the trial, three weeks earlier, with just a handful of journalists in the overflow annexe, while I sat alone in the main room. The public gallery, though, was as full as ever, some of the faces as familiar now as the journalists and lawyers who had been there throughout, though others were new, like a well-dressed, middle-aged woman who came through the security checks behind me. She said she had never been inside a court before but had come to listen to Karen and Mick's trial, having seen it on the news and 'thought it looked quite interesting.'

The feeling in Court 12 was one of finality. The air of excitement and anticipation had gone, temporarily - it would certainly return in the moments leading up to the verdict - everyone there knew that the time for jaw-dropping revelations was past. The lawyers would now sum up their cases, marshalling their strongest arguments, the defence trying to plant seeds of doubt in the jurors' minds while the prosecution sought to eradicate them.

With the ritual two sharp raps on the door, the judge walked in, quite quickly, and took his place in his high-backed, red leather seat. The High Sheriff walked in ahead of him, while another notably dressed figure was behind, a bespectacled, balding man, wearing a long black dress coat, white kerchief in pocket, a blue-pinstripe shirt with detachable white collar, and a white, cravat-style tie. While the Sheriff carried a sword, the newcomer had a long, thin, highly polished wooden rod, topped with a small metal spike. He propped the object in a corner, and, unexplained, took his seat on the judge's left. The judge waited while everyone settled in their places and then allowed Mrs Oldham to begin her final address to the seven men and five women who would decide her client's fate.

In contrast to Karen's less-than-inspiring performance in the witness box, her QC's speech to the jury was sparkling. Perhaps surprisingly - though, given Karen's changing stories and the verbal ribbons that Messrs Goose and Conrad had cut her into, it was probably unavoidable - Mrs Oldham began by conceding that her client might have lied at some points in the inquiry. However, said Mrs Oldham, the prosecution's case was fatally flawed and a flawed defendant did not mean the case was proven. She pointed to the way that Mr Goose had asked the jurors to believe Mick's evidence about the plan, but then told them not to believe his claims about acting under threat of violence from Karen. 'On the one hand the prosecution says he (Mick) is reliable, on the other hand they say he is a liar,' Mrs Oldham said.

She also highlighted the statement read to the court, from Donovan's sister, Maria Harper, saying that her brother was a fantasist and capable of making stories up about 'anything and everything'. Mrs Oldham highlighted the gaps she claimed to see in the prosecution's case, and stressed to the jury that there was no evidence whatsoever to link Karen to the inside of Mick's flat - no DNA, no fingerprints - and the only evidence connecting her to the outside was one possible sighting, of no more than thirty seconds, made late at night by a woman who admitted she could not be sure it was Karen.

Mrs Oldham regularly used the phrase 'it does not make sense', as she sought to plant the necessary doubt in the minds of the jury. Holding eye-contact with each juror in turn, she spoke to them in a calm, unemotional voice with no theatrics or histrionics, laying out her version of events as matter-of-factly as a finance director presenting the company accounts at the annual general meeting. If her delivery was deadpan, her language was rich at times, including words and phrases rarely heard in common usage, like 'vis-à-vis' and even the Shakespearean 'betwixt', though she did adopt a more populist tone when trying to rubbish the idea that Karen and Mick had planned to swindle the media out of £50,000. 'They would be giving lessons to the likes of Max Clifford,' she said.

Mrs Oldham had some respectful words for Julie Bushby, describing her as 'sensible, sound, grounded, and no-nonsense,' before bringing the speech back to Mick's character and reliability as a witness. She asked the jury to consider what his agenda was and whether they could rely on his evidence enough to be able to convict her client. 'If you cannot be sure, then I respectfully suggest the verdict must be "Not Guilty",' she said, before resuming her seat.

Through it all, Karen had stared straight ahead, hands folded in her lap, listening intently, while Mick was frozen like a statue, staring at a spot where the wooden dock joined the plastic screen attached to it, while a staff member from his solicitor's offices did his best to guide Mick through what was being said.

Neither defendant changed their position as Mr Goose summed up for the prosecution. Karen did not even flinch when Mr Goose told the jury that she had 'lied and lied and lied again', the contradictions beginning soon after she made the 999 call to report Shannon missing. The prosecutor again stressed to the jurors how many times Karen had changed her story, the contradictions in the five different versions she used, eventually leaving her with no further options. 'She has lied, we say, so often and so much that she has reached the point where all she can say is "I was confused", and then blame everyone else except herself. She is, as we said at the beginning of this trial, a consummate liar.'

Mr Goose said it was those lies that had caught Karen out, as the inconsistencies from the different stories she had told had left her exposed to the emerging truth. He told the jury: 'You know, as we all do from life experiences, that people who tell lies have to stick to the lie because if they change it they get found out. You may think, ladies and gentleman, as you can be sure about it, she has been found out for the dishonest and, we say, wicked liar that she is. Ladies and gentlemen, this was a plan between Karen Matthews and Michael Donovan. It was a plan to take Shannon and keep her captive and make a false complaint, wait for the reward money to grow, pretend to find her and then claim the money. That was the plan between them.'

Mr Conrad, representing Mick, then rose to his feet, used his closing speech to try and paint Mick as someone who was not only incapable of standing up for himself but also of planning and executing a kidnap plot. His client was not an 'evil monster,' Mr Conrad said, but was instead 'pathetic, inadequate . . . vulnerable, unsophisticated and weak in body and mind.'

Adopting a different tone from when he was cross-examining - reassuring and persuasive where before he had been sceptical and hectoring - Mr Conrad urged the seven men and five women to take care not to let their emotions influence their ability to sift through the evidence and reach a verdict. 'There was a young child in this case. You may think a number of people involved in this case have been influenced by emotion, a number of people including police witnesses,' he said.

It was a reminder to the jury of an allegation that Mr Conrad had repeatedly made throughout the trial. He claimed that the two detectives and the uniformed search team who had broken into and searched Mick's flat and found Shannon had let their emotions get the better of them, had sworn at and assaulted Mick, and had exchanged 'high-five' celebrations outside 26 Lidgate Gardens when Shannon was safe.

However those allegations were flatly denied by the officers involved. Some of them had described the way Shannon was found as 'surreal', and two of them, parents themselves, admitted they had felt some emotion after finding a missing girl after 24 days, but all strongly rejected any accusations of violence or improper behaviour.

Developing his theme, Mr Conrad said that we now lived in 'curious' times, surrounded by reality television and people wanting their fifteen minutes of fame. He told the jury the case was a 'symptom' of the times, as it was alleged the kidnap plot involved claiming a £50,000 reward put forward by a national newspaper.

The police officers, Mr Conrad claimed, had allowed their emotions to affect them, and that their evidence was 'riddled with inaccuracies'. They were playing to the gallery, Mr Conrad claimed. 'They have tried to cover themselves in glory,' he told the jury. 'This was their fifteen minutes of fame and they have singularly failed.'

With all three counsels' closing speeches complete, the judge gave the jury a short break, and even inquired after the health of one woman juror, who had developed a hacking cough, before beginning the process of summing up the evidence. Mr Justice McCombe now faced the complex and tiring task of running through the most important points of more than three weeks of evidence, drawing on the page after page of notes he had taken while the barristers had the floor.

The jurors sat listening to him intently, while Karen and Mick kept the same posture they had adopted during the closing speeches. The barristers, sitting directly in front of the judge, sat bolt upright, paying close attention and occasionally making brief notes. The people in the public galleries seemed less attentive, perhaps eager for this phase of the trial to be over, so that the real drama; the jury's exit and later return to announce the verdict, could begin.

After more than a full court day summing up the evidence, the judge finally invited the jurors to retire to consider their verdict. He advised them that, for now, he wanted a unanimous verdict, but would call them back into court should that position change and a majority become acceptable. With that, the jury bailiff took the oath and the twelve members of that ancient British institution, the jury, filed silently out through the side door, to decide the fates of Karen Matthews and Michael Donovan.

CHAPTER 48

AFTER DAYS, WEEKS, OR SOMETIMES EVEN MONTHS of activity, a trial enters a strange state of limbo while the jury is considering its verdict. Everything slows, almost to a stop, like an animal going into hibernation. The judge and the lawyers vanish, the judge to his or her chambers, the barristers presumably to the robing rooms, and everyone else is left to mill about and kill the time as best they can.

There is a civilised convention of letting everyone know that no verdict will be returned during the lunch adjournment, but otherwise people have to hang around in the waiting area outside the courtroom, drinking endless cups of tea and coffee in the canteen, or, for those who came prepared, flicking through newspapers or getting stuck into that book that has been waiting, unread, by the side of the bed.

The Shannon trial was slightly different, in that, because of the large numbers of press and public there, the court managers decided to keep the overflow room open while the jury was out, though the doors to Court 12, where the 'live' action had taken place, remained firmly locked. The annexe, as it had become known, had five flat-screen televisions and two huge speakers set up on the judge's bench, in front of the beige drapes with the lion and unicorn crest and the legend 'Dieu et Mon Droit'. In front of the bench, the three banks of seating usually used by lawyers had been taken over by journalists and transformed into a mini-newsroom, with laptops, notebooks, dog-eared newspapers and abandoned biros scattered across them. Now and again a mobile phone would ring. It sounded extremely out-of-place in a courtroom, one of the world's last mobile-free zones and a place where, in theory at least, the owner of a ringing phone could be sent to the cells on the spot, for contempt of court. Fortunately for the media workers, the 'no-phones' rule had been relaxed in the annexe, though not in the court room itself.

Up to forty journalists, of all ages and careers, were now killing time in there, waiting for the jury to complete its work. The unofficial pecking order among journalists was partly reflected in the seating arrangements. A small group of reporters for the national newspapers sat together towards the front of the benches, bashing away at their laptop keyboards, occasionally laughing loudly at a remembered and shared anecdote. Behind them, three broadcast journalists, one radio, two television, chatted quietly, while to their left, two Press Association staff, some of journalism's biggest workhorses, went through their notes in detail, checking everything was in place for the huge background pieces they would send out as soon as the verdict was in. Behind them, the rear benches were occupied by reporters for the local newspapers.

Even the dock, a place where many people would no doubt like to see journalists end up, had been made available for extra seating, and two television reporters were sitting there, one leafing through Now magazine, the other rubbing his eyes as he checked messages on a Blackberry. Meanwhile the Yorkshire Post's Olwen Dudgeon, one of the best-known faces at Leeds Crown Court, buzzed around, keeping herself busy, and the court usher, the lynchpin of a hearing, always there to make sure all runs smoothly, had taken off his long black robes, and was sitting back, enjoying a rare moment of repose, waiting patiently and occasionally stroking his beard.

The clock ticked slowly on to a point in the late afternoon where few, if any, of the press pack would have welcomed a verdict, leaving them trying to conduct interviews and cobble together background pieces on the coldest, darkest night of the year so far. When the closed circuit television screens sprang into life and the judge declared that he planned to send the jury home for the night, the sighs of weariness were replaced by those of relief. The suspense would continue for at least one more day.

CHAPTER 49

IF THE WEATHER WAS THREATENING on the day the jury retired to consider its verdict, by the second day of their deliberations the elements were doing their best to derail the trial. Several centimetres of snow fell overnight and Leeds city centre, gridlocked with traffic at the best of times, was temporarily brought to a complete standstill. The judge's plans for a 10am start had to be put on hold, as two jury members were struggling to make it into court; given the conditions, it was a surprise that so few were late. As I arrived at court, I cast a sympathetic glance towards the photographers huddled outside, shuffling backwards and forwards through the snow and slush like emperor penguins on an Antarctic ice floe, as they waited to catch the more notable arrivals and departures from the courts for what might prove to be the last time on the Matthews' trial.

When I got through security, Peter, the ever-helpful usher in the overflow annexe, indicated the official start had been put back to 11am, shrugging as he did so to say that even that should not be taken as read. 'We're waiting to wait,' a Crown Prosecution Service press officer, said with a smile, meaning that even when proceedings did start, it would only mean that we could resume waiting for the verdict.

At eleven o'clock a start was made as the microphones in the annexe crackled with sound and the television screens flashed into life. The jury bailiffs re-swore the oaths: 'I shall keep this jury in a private and convenient place, I shall not offer any person to speak to them, nor shall any person speak to them about the trial unless it is about the verdict, so help you God,' before the seven men and five women again filed noiselessly out, ready to take their discussions into the fifth hour.

The faces on the press benches looked fresher this time, reaping the benefits of a new day and night's sleep, and the annexe was alive with atmosphere and anticipation again, the hot topic being the rigorous terms of a new, high-court injunction, banning the publication of any detail whatsoever that might lead to the identification of any of Karen's children. A group of national newspaper staffers already had their heads together, debating the worth of a legal challenge against the ruling.

I spent much of the morning in the press room, working on other news stories, though my mind was only half on that. Paranoid that I might miss the call to return to court for the climax of the case as the jurors returned, I kept poking my head out of the door to scan the waiting area, checking that my colleagues were still milling around. At last, at about 12.40pm, the PA system crackled into life with the announcement we had all been waiting for: 'Could all parties in the case of Karen Matthews and Michael Donovan please make their way to Court 12.'

I leapt to my feet as though an electric current had shot through the keys of my laptop and hurriedly closed it down. In my haste and excitement I was clumsy and fumbling as I tried to put my laptop back in its case, and had to take a deep breath and remind myself that I had at least five minutes to spare, before I could free the zip and close the case.

A queue of spectators was waiting outside the still-locked doors of Court 12. The trial's QCs politely muttering 'excuse me,' as they eased their way through them to make their way in. A detective then appeared, warning those waiting against any misbehaviour in court during the reading of the verdict. 'I know feelings are running high,' he said, 'But if there is any carrying on, you will be thrown out from the court.'

That confirmed it - a decision had been reached one way or the other - and I squeezed a quick call into my news-desk to tip them off. I'd already turned off my phone, ready to go into court, and it seemed to take an age to switch on, though in reality it was no slower than normal. I heard the phone ringing and ringing, before the voice of

Tony Harney, the YEP's deputy news editor, growled 'Hello, news-desk.'

Somehow, he already knew what was coming, saying 'Any time now is it, Richard?' calm as you like.

'Yeah, we've got a verdict, be on standby,' I burbled, the excitement building and adrenaline pumping through my veins.

As we filed into Court 12, I was surprised to see a few spare seats in the public area, though the press benches were jam-packed full. By now I was buzzing with anticipation so much that I could hardly keep still. BBC Look North's John Cundy, a man who has seen dozens of big verdicts in his time, was sitting next to me, and shared at least some of my excitement. 'No matter how many of these you do,' he said, 'you still feel the butterflies.'

Detective Constables Alex Grummitt and Christine Freeman, the family liaison officers who had spent more time with Karen than any other officers, were sitting behind us, and I saw Detective Superintendent Andy Brennan in his usual spot, to the far left of the room, a few feet behind the witness box. As we waited, the atmosphere was so tense you could almost reach up, grab a bit and bottle it away for later.

Suddenly we heard the ritual two raps on the door and Mr Justice McCombe made his entrance. Then there was the jangling of a key, sounding louder than ever in the tense, silent court. The door leading from the holding cells to the dock opened, and Karen and Mick were shown in. Karen nodded to the dock officer as he gestured towards her usual seat, Mick had his head bowed, as always, sitting down slowly and deliberately.

The judge added his own warning to that issued by the detective outside the courtroom. 'Whatever the verdict may be, can I ask that it is treated properly, and with respect, and I do not expect anybody rushing out of court (when it has been delivered.)' He looked at the press benches as he said those last few words, a reminder to anyone with a looming deadline that they would have to wait an extra minute or two while the sombre business of the court was concluded.

The judge then shifted his gaze to the dock. 'Right, Karen Matthews and Michael Donovan, stand up please.' When they had got to their feet, the clerk of the court asked the jury if they had elected a foreman, and if so, could he or she please stand up. A man in his early thirties, with short brown hair and wearing a brown pullover got to his feet. Face grave, he confirmed that the jurors had reached a verdict on which they were all agreed.

Time seemed to slow down as the clerk then read the charges: kidnapping, false imprisonment and perverting the course of justice. The air was thick with anticipation, some eyes on the foreman, others on the dock, the clerk asking first what the verdict was on Mick, and then Karen. Each time he put the question, the answer was the same: 'Guilty'. The jury foreman spoke quietly, but without evident nerves, as he repeated the same word six times in all.

Without realising it, I'd been holding my breath as he gave the verdicts and I let it out in a long exhalation as the foreman sat down. Everything was back to normal speed now, quicker, if anything, reporters struggling to write fast enough. It was a momentous verdict: the jury were unanimous in their agreement that both defendants were guilty of all three serious charges that had been laid before them. The woman standing before them had recruited an accomplice with the plan of using her own nine-year-old child to swindle a few thousand pounds out of a newspaper. It was a plan breathtaking in both its naked greed and its stupidity, doomed to failure from the moment it was hatched.

Those with their eyes on Karen and Mick, convicted criminals now, no longer defendants, were perhaps disappointed that the guilty verdicts, damning both of them to many years behind bars, were received without a flicker of emotion, their bodies stock still, with not even a blink of an eye in recognition, Karen kept staring grimly ahead, Mick looked vacantly at his usual spot a foot or so off the floor.

Often, at the end of long, expensive and high-profile trials, the judge will move quickly to the sentence, but in this case he decided that pre-sentence reports were needed, saying that while he had heard much about the psychology of the two, and particularly about Mick, he needed to know more about their background and the lives they had led before the crime they had committed. However, he concluded with a comment that must have eliminated any last shreds of hope that Karen or Mick might have been nurturing. Looking straight at them, though both kept their gaze averted from his, Justice McCombe warned them, 'It must be said, there are likely to be substantial custodial sentences.' With that, he nodded to the dock officers, 'They can be taken down now.'

Karen and Mick still appeared impassive as they were led away. Now two of Britain's most notorious criminals, I did not envy them their fate: targets in jail and figures of hate, vilified in the tabloid press. The door of the dock clicked shut behind them, a muted contrast to the slamming steel prison doors and gates that they would be hearing many times every day in the long years ahead.

With the defendants gone, the press were straining at the leash to be off and filing their reports, but the judge took the time to thank the jury for their commitment and punctuality, the barristers for their efficiency, and the court staff, particularly the clerk and the usher, for their dedication and professionalism, before adjourning the case for sentence. Press and public showed the respect he had requested, walking slowly and soundlessly away, as Detective Superintendent Brennan gave Detective Constable Freeman a kiss on the cheek and quietly said, 'Well done'. Their pleasure at the successful outcome to such a long, complex and incredibly challenging case was entirely understandable.

In the foyer, Julie Bushby and Petra Jamieson spoke of their confusion, saying that Karen remained a friend and that they would visit her, though perhaps just once, depending on her reaction, if only to ask 'Why?' A hundred cameras flashed as the two women, with

Julie's daughter, Tiffany, Natalie Brown and her husband Peter walked out of the court, into the sleet and the slush. Detective Superintendent Brennan followed a short time later, and paused to make a short statement to the press. He spoke of how, for the sake of money, Shannon had been betrayed by her mother, the woman she was supposed to be able to trust above all others in the world. 'Karen's interest and motivation throughout this has not been for Shannon or anybody else, it's been for her and getting her hands on £50,000.'

Detective Superintendent Brennan also revealed for the first time just how much the intense pressure to find the missing nine-year-old had affected his near-400 strong search team. He told reporters: 'At times we almost reached breaking point. The vast majority of staff and officers were parents or grandparents themselves. They didn't need anyone to remind them of the consequences of not finding Shannon. On the day she was found alive, everyone was in tears. I've never seen an incident room like it. It was a very emotional time.'

After that, it was time for me to slip away, my court reporting colleague Mark Lavery kindly agreeing to cover for me, as I had the following day's front page to write and final checks on an eight-page Shannon special, which Bruce Smith and I had written, before making a final trip to Dewsbury Moor.

CHAPTER 50

THE YEP'S NEWSROOM WAS BUZZING. The televisions in the newsroom were all tuned to rolling news stations, and all of them were showing acres of coverage of the Shannon case now that the reporting restrictions imposed during the trial had been lifted. Bruce was speaking to his police contacts before heading to a briefing in Leeds's famous pub, The Victoria, where he had arranged to collect background DVDs on Karen and Mick that the West Yorkshire Police had prepared. I wrote my story as quickly as I could, News Editor Gillian Haworth shuttling between my desk and hers as we agreed on the approach to take, while editor Paul Napier worked with the sub-editors on the layout of the special edition. Colleagues, as fascinated as everyone else by the case, kept coming over, wanting to hear how it had gone at court, and asking a couple of questions before backing away, knowing the deadline was looming.

Job done, with a thumbs-up from Gillian, it was time to gather my kit - four bags with laptop computer, video camera, tripod and general kitbag, the regular burden of the modern news reporter. Then I headed for the Moor to see for myself how the community was coping as it came under the microscope yet again. There was still snow and ice underfoot and as I took that well-travelled route, there was a crown of icy snow atop the bronze Billy Bremner's head outside Elland Road. It was now late afternoon, and the watery winter sun was low in the sky. As I drove along, my mobile phone kept buzzing like an angry bee as a flurry of text and voicemail messages dropped in, national news outlets wanting a local man's view on the final act in this near year-long drama.

The streets of the estate were quiet, most people inside sheltering from the cold, My usual spot, outside the community house, was free, some unfamiliar faces peering out, one of them, a woman in a police-style fluorescent jacket, not looking pleased to see yet another reporter, but then most of the people there probably wanted nothing more than to be left alone to get on with their lives. After one last flurry of attention, their wish would be granted and the media circus would move on to the next big story, wherever that might be. As I stood outside the community house, one by one people started to appear, their clothing so dark against the snowy backdrop, that at a distance they looked like ants crawling across a page of A4 paper.

I spoke to several of them, and though Mick largely seemed to be forgotten in the general condemnation, their message about Karen was loud and clear: she was a disgrace, if kidnap carries a life sentence the judge should hand it down and life should mean life.

When I got to Moorside Road it was busier, with half-a-dozen television satellite vans parked on the verge and BBC Look North's Harry Gration and Christa Ackroyd preparing to do live link-ups from outside number 24. There was the constant noise of phones buzzing, while a scattering of local children, aged about ten, hoods pulled up against the cold, kicked a ball around and rode their bikes in among the journalists and their equipment.

Julie Bushby, much in demand from the media, dealt with all the calls in her usual no-nonsense way, and there were plenty of requests too, for the thoughts of Petra Jamieson and Natalie Brown, those three, strong local women, so central to the once-quiet community caught up in a media whirlwind. I found Natalie's husband, Peter, sitting quietly in his house, watching the Shannon coverage, and he shared with me his reflections on one of the strangest years of his life, praising the spirit his neighbours had shown and the dedication of the police team who had eventually brought Shannon home. 'It's still all sinking in,' he said. 'I think it'll take a while. But it does feel like a weight is starting to lift off our shoulders.'

Back outside, I paused at the junction of Moorside Avenue and Moorside Road, the sun, brighter now and shining through some clouds, as it slipped quickly towards the horizon. I thought about what Peter had said, the heavy load beginning to lift from this once anonymous corner of West Yorkshire. In time, the cool wind blowing down from the Pennines might blow away the dirt that stuck to this community during the long ten months that had gone before. I hoped that even when their anger and hurt at the way that Karen Matthews had betrayed her children and her community had faded, the Moor's residents would never forget that, when the world's gaze was upon them, they did themselves proud, and can forever hold their heads high.

APPENDIX

THE MAIN CHARACTERS

SHANNON MATTHEWS

Little is known about the girl who, at one point, appeared to have vanished from the face of the earth. Shannon is the second oldest of Karen's seven children, and, until she was placed at the centre of a global news story, lived the life of any other young child in a low-income family on a council estate.

She liked to spend time in her bedroom, which she shared with younger sister, playing with her beloved Bratz dolls. Many people will remember the description of the Bratz boots she was wearing on the day she disappeared.

Sources within West Yorkshire Police have said that, understandably, Shannon's recollection of what went on during those days in Mick's flat is confused. She had little contact with her mother in the days between being found in the bottom of Mick's divan bed and Karen being arrested, and she was not called as a witness during her mother's trial, partly because her evidence might not be reliable, but mainly because of the immense stress it would have placed on her, even if she had spoken through a videolink.

Shannon is now ten-years-old. Where she lives remains a closely guarded secret.

KAREN MATTHEWS

Until February 2008, Karen Matthews was just another unmarried mother living a deprived life on a housing estate. Then her bungled kidnap conspiracy changed her life forever.

Dewsbury is Karen's home town, Dewsbury Moor her home estate. She was born in Dewsbury, has lived there all her life, and has rarely ventured far from home. It was an uncomplicated background, and, despite her tangled web of past relationships, Karen led an essentially uncomplicated home life. Before her arrest, four of her children lived with her and live-in partner Craig Meehan, a set-up that, despite some media portrayals of her, was pretty close to that of a nuclear family. Her life centred on her home; apart from trips into Dewsbury or Heckmondwike, she spent the rest of her time in her Moorside Road home or those of friends living nearby.

Karen was born in 1975. Her parents, June and Gordon Matthews, were traditional, working class people. Gordon worked in that staple of Dewsbury area industry, Fox's Biscuit Factory, while June was employed in the textile trade. June had seven children, five boys and two girls, and both her daughters would go on to do the same.

The eldest girl, Julie, remained married to the same man, but Karen, Julie's younger sister by five years, has had several failed relationships, her last, the four-year link-up with Craig, said to be the longest of them. Shannon is the second oldest of Karen's seven children to six different fathers.

Why Karen should have moved from man to man is unclear, but former friends say she had claimed to have been a victim of sexual abuse during her childhood. One Dewsbury Moor resident, who knows her well, said: 'She said she had been an abuse victim, and of course it is possible. But Karen lies, she always has and she always will, so it's hard to know if she is lying about that or not.'

Karen's cousin, Susan Howgate, said she had never heard her

cousin make such a claim. 'She has never said that to me,' Mrs Howgate said. 'I don't know why she had so many partners, maybe she just didn't find the right person. She thought she had done with Craig.'

Mrs Howgate, who spent hours trawling the Dewsbury streets with her husband Graham and their dog, hoping to find a trace of Shannon, added, 'She got everybody on her side and then we found out she had lied about it. She deserves everything she gets.'

MICHAEL DONOVAN

Until March 14 this year, few people had heard of Michael, or Mick, Donovan. Despite his relative closeness, at least in family terms, as the uncle of Shannon's step-dad, the police had not yet knocked on his door, and Shannon's family members made no mention of him during the 24 days she was away from home.

Born Paul Drake in 1968, Mick was one of several children of Marian and Joseph Drake. One of his sisters was Craig Meehan's mother, Alice, who has rarely spoken about him. When she did mention him, she said, separated by a ten-year age gap, they were not close, and living on different sides of Dewsbury, rarely had any contact with each other. When asked about Mick after Shannon's rescue, Mrs Meehan simply shuddered and said, 'He is my so-called brother,' before declining to comment further.

It appears that Mick began to suffer mental health problems quite early in life. He always had a passion for driving, investing in more than 100 lessons before he was to pass his test, later securing a job as a professional driver, but by the time of the Shannon saga he was living alone and surviving on disability benefits.

Neighbours at his home in Lidgate Gardens, Batley Carr, spoke of a loner, a man who was rarely seen out and about and who spoke to few of his neighbours when he was seen. He was apparently very proud of his car, and would spend long periods cleaning and polishing it. Neighbours knew that he very rarely left home without his car, and so were able to tell police officers that Mick was there when they called at his home and got no answer. Minutes later, they rescued Shannon. It is thought that Mick already knew Shannon, the youngster having taken a shine to him at a family function, and that he had rowed with Karen and Craig over their care for the girl. It is understood Mick was once married, and had two daughters. The children do not live with either of their parents and he does not have access to them.

Michael Donovan told his trial jury that the reason he changed his name from Paul Drake was because of his love for the 1980s science-fiction series V, and its lead character, Mike Donovan. He said he liked "action heroes" and that his original name had led to him being bullied at school. A former neighbour, however, told the trial that she believed the name change was down to him being a big fan of Jason Donovan.

As he was led away from his flat by the officers who found him and Shannon, cowering in a divan bed, Mick turned to neighbours and said, 'Don't hate me – I'm a poorly man.'

In the run-up to his court appearances, it was revealed that during police interviews, Donovan's grasp on the proceedings was so poor he had to have an appropriate adult with him. Usually only children aged under 18 have to be accompanied by an adult. The man who sat hunched in the dock during his trial, his gaze flitting around the courtroom, his attention seeming distracted, did not look to be a man of forty. Instead, his thin, broken figure, and gaunt, twisted features, were those of a man at least twenty-five years his senior.

CRAIG MEEHAN

Craig Meehan appeared to be an unlikely partner for Karen Matthews. Ten years her junior, he moved in with a woman who already had six children by five different fathers. On the face of it, Karen was the dominant one in the relationship. Craig's appearance, his blank expression and thick-lensed spectacles gave many people the impression that he was of lower-than-average intelligence. But the way he looked masked a more complex personality. More articulate than he appeared, the former supermarket fishmonger was the brighter of the two, and able to read and write more confidently than his former partner.

His trial at the Magistrates' Court saw Craig reveal considerable technical knowledge of the workings of computers and the internet, knowledge he used to try to cover his tracks when downloading child pornography. But the plan to stage Shannon's disappearance, cooked up by his uncle and his partner proved to be his undoing, as the Shannon inquiry team seized his computer in the search for clues to the schoolgirl's whereabouts. They hoped to find a hint on a social networking site, or perhaps an email Shannon had sent to a friend. Instead, detectives uncovered dozens of child porn images, some of them at the most serious end of the scale.

Craig Meehan denied any wrongdoing to the end, challenging the Crown's case in court and taking a combative, even aggressive style in the witness box. But the district judge hearing the case found his evidence unreliable, and convicted him of eleven offences relating to the possession of child pornography. He was sentenced to twenty weeks in jail, but was released because of the time he had already served on remand. Former neighbours in Dewsbury Moor warned him not to come back, and his current whereabouts are unknown.

NEIL AND AMANDA HYETT

Amanda is Craig Meehan's older sister. Her husband, Neil, is a bus and coach driver, and they have three children. Neil and Amanda live just yards away from Shannon's former home, and they played a central role in the search for Shannon, helping to print and distribute leaflets and showing some skill in the way they handled the media.

Amanda was hit hard in the first week in April, when four members of her family were arrested. Craig was picked up first over the child porn inquiry, then, after allegations made by Mick to police, Amanda, her sister Caroline and mother Alice were all arrested, though the three women were all later released without charge.

Amanda broke down in court when Craig was convicted of the child porn charges, and, although she condemned what he did, said she had to stand by him for family reasons.

ALICE MEEHAN

Alice Meehan is the mother of Craig and Amanda, and Shannon knew her as her grandma. Widowed in 2007, she lives a short distance away from Moorside Road, but kept a low profile during Shannon's time away from home. She had little contact with her brother Mick, ten years younger than her, although she said he supported her well in the time after her husband's death and through his funeral, before they again became estranged.

Alice had little time for Karen, believing her son could do better for himself. She mainly kept this to herself, but spoke out when articles appeared in which Karen's mother, June, was heavily critical of Craig.

She stood by her son despite his child porn convictions, and was in the back of the police car with him as he was whisked away to a safe house following the court's verdict. Alice has talked Craig out of suicide at least once since the end of his trial.

JULIE BUSHBY

Julie is not related to the Matthews or Meehan families. Until Shannon vanished, Julie did not know Karen well, but then threw the support and resources of the Moorside Tenants' and Residents' Association behind the search, helping to co-ordinate it, dealing confidently and competently with the media, and turning the Moorside Avenue community house into the headquarters of the Search for Shannon campaign.

A mother of three, Julie is a solid, no-nonsense Yorkshirewoman who gets things done and is popular on Dewsbury Moor for her commitment to the community and willingness to stand up for it.

PETER AND NATALIE BROWN

Like Julie, neither Peter nor Natalie are related to Shannon's family. Their role, like most of the neighbours, was to help and support, Neil Hyett once describing Peter as 'my right hand man' when the search was at its height. Peter, a former soldier, was also once close to Craig, saying they had been best mates, and Craig's arrest and conviction left him deeply shocked.

Natalie helped bring the whole saga to an end, working with Julie to question Karen after the two women became suspicious about her behaviour. That questioning led to Karen breaking down and confessing.

The couple adopted Shannon's dog, Scania, after 24 Moorside Road was left empty when Craig and Karen were arrested within four days of each other.